Giftocracy

Giftocracy

Awakening the Seeds of Greatness

Michael Tetteh

Made for Grace
PUBLISHING

Made For Grace Publishing
P.O. Box 1775 Issaquah, WA 98027
www.MadeForGrace.com

Distributed by Made For Grace Publishing
Managing editor: Alice Sullivan, alicesullivan.com
Copy editor: Shayla Eaton, curiousediting.com

Cover Design by DeeDee Heathman
Interior Design by DeeDee Heathman

Library of Congress Cataloging-in-Publication data
Tetteh, Michael
     Giftocracy: Awakening the Seeds of Greatness
     p. cm.
     ISBN: 9781613397497
     LCCN: 2015945893

For further information contact Made For Grace Publishing +14255266480 or email service@madeforsuccess.net

Printed in the United States of America

ENDORSEMENTS

"God created each of us with unique gifts to be used for His great Kingdom's purposes. With the power of his own personal story, my friend Michael Tetteh has a challenging message in this book that will inspire you to discover your gift and pursue your purpose with passion."

—Richard Stearns, President of World Vision US, Author of *Unfinished* and *The Hole in Our Gospel*

"In a world filled with aimlessness, Michael gives us a gift: the possibility of clarity, calling, and purpose. In a world filled with fear, Michael gives us a gift: the possibility of living courageously. In a world filled with greed, Michael gives us a gift: the possibility of living generously and joyously with open hands. Michael's story is more than an inspiration; it's a gift offered for anyone looking to fill their one precious life with meaning."

—Richard Dahlstrom, Senior Pastor of Bethany Community Church, Seattle, Author of *The Colors of Hope: Becoming People of Mercy, Justice, and Love*

"Michael Tetteh's story packs a punch. This is a book which shapes the mindset of leaders."
—**Bryan Heathman, Author of *Conversion Marketing: Convert Website Visitors to Buyers***

"*Giftocracy* is about the very idea that we have all been blessed with natural gifts and talents. When fully activated, these will lead us into opportunities, experiences, and successes that all of the things we used to chase never could. It is simply about realizing that the gift inside you is what holds the key to your successful future."
—**Steve Zakuani,   Former Seattle Sounder Star, Author of *500 Days* and Founder of Kingdom Hope**

"We have heard of the American Dream, but not so much of God's dream for His people. Michael's life has proven that no matter where you come from— even if it is extreme poverty—if you draw close to God and discover the amazing gifts He has given all of us, you can beat insurmountable odds. Michael's life and book should inspire all of us that if *he can* do it, *we can* all enjoy God's intended blessings for those who call on His name. I am blessed to have Michael working for me, and after forty-plus years in the fitness business, he is one of the most amazing people I have ever met. His story, his book will bless you, and most of all inspire you."
—**Neil Schober, Author of *Strawberry Fields Forever*, Owner of Emerald City Athletics**

DEDICATION

To anyone who has ever been labeled as different and who has the stamina and fortitude to dance to the beat of a different drum.

To my fellow Africans, whom I urge to emancipate from the expectations and opinions of others, defy the standards of success created by the powers that be, and feel empowered to dissociate yourself with the status quo and forge your own God-given gifts. Refuse to identify yourselves with the lifestyles and preferences established by others. I encourage you to decide today to be yourself, discover your gift, and serve it to your generation.

To those from countries deemed to be the "Third World" who desire to maximize their full potential and embrace a life of purpose characterized by effectiveness, true success, and fulfillment. May this book be a source of inspiration for you. May the stories in this book—including my personal story—empower you to discover your gift and serve that gift to the world. It is my deepest hope that you will meet your true self.

CONTENTS

PART THREE
Give: The Meaning of Life is to Give Your Gift Away

"The purpose of life is to discover your gift. The work of life is to develop it. Th meaning of life is to give your gift away."

—David Viscott

FOREWORD

I'm willing to bet that no human has ever woken up in the morning and said to themselves, "I can't wait to see how badly I can fail today!" The desire for success is natural to the human spirit. Even though we go about pursuing it in different ways, all seven billion of us want to be successful. We want to feel significant; we want our lives to matter. Why then do so few of us attain success? Very few people can honestly say that they are as successful as they would want to be, or as successful as they can be. I believe the reason very few of us attain success, even though it's something we all want, is because we have been pursuing success incorrectly.

We've been taught that success lies in the next promotion, the next car, the next house, the next guy or girl we meet, the next paycheck, the next job, the next degree, or the next...you get the point. And so we end up in this cycle of constantly seeking for things *outside of ourselves* to fulfill us or to give us value. And as I'm sure you know by now, that cycle is never ending, and it never allows you to become successful enough to be truly fulfilled. Success does not come from pursuing something outside of ourselves; but rather it comes from a realization that everything we need to be successful and fulfilled has always been right inside us. Don't look externally for success and fulfillment, for the seeds of success are already inside you.

In this book, Michael Tetteh captures this philosophy perfectly. *Giftocracy* is about the very idea that we have all been blessed with natural gifts and talents. When fully activated, these will lead us into opportunities, experiences, and success that all of the things we used to chase never could. *Giftocracy* is simply about realizing that the gift inside you is what holds the key to your successful future.

I met Michael a few years ago when he was drafted to play with the Seattle Sounders, the Major League Soccer team I was already on. Knowing he was from Africa originally, like me, made me go out of my way to make sure he felt welcome in our locker room right away. He was a good player, but I sensed from the very beginning that his life would become about more than soccer. My premonition would prove to be correct.

Michael quickly realized that soccer was merely the springboard that would launch him into the next phase of his life, which was to share his story about using his gifts to rise from poverty to genuine success and fulfillment. Some people only talk about wanting success, while other people are prepared to give their last breath to its pursuit. Michael is in the second group.

During his two years with me on the Sounders, I did with him what I had done with many people before. I mentored him on and off the pitch. By mentoring, I really mean *challenged*. I challenged him to be better: a better player, a better man, a better human being. I read a lot of uplifting books and so I routinely handed books to Michael that I was reading, and then quizzed him on what he had learned once he read them. We went out to dinner regularly and talked for hours on end about purpose, leadership, and life in general. I pushed him to dream big, to embrace a noble cause in life, and to inspire those around him not by what he said, but by *how he lived*.

The demands I made on him were the same demands a mentor had made on me years earlier when I had reached a crossroads in my life. Though many people I have mentored in the past told me to back off—as they realized it is much easier to go with the crowd and be normal than to be challenged and pushed to become someone exceptional who stands out—Michael not only embraced the challenge, but he also took it to a new level.

I no longer needed to hand him my books; he bought his own. I didn't have to initiate our thought-provoking conversations; he did. I watched him grow. And I watched him stop looking to others for validation and stop seeking their permission to be great. He began to understand Giftocracy. He began to understand that his success was already within him and that the rest of his life was simply about letting his gift take him to places where he could serve and inspire.

The mentor who changed my life once told me, "I will not be satisfied until you are more successful than I am." I finally understand what he meant. When you choose to mentor someone—that is a serious investment. And let me tell you, there is nothing better than seeing a positive return on your investment. When it comes to mentoring, the best investment is seeing your mentee out-succeed you. *Giftocracy* is Michael's first step toward out-succeeding me, and I couldn't be more proud.

—Steve Zakuani, Former Seattle Sounder Star, Author of
500 Days and Founder of Kingdom Hope

YOUR GIFT IS WRAPPED. ARE YOU READY TO UNWRAP IT?

Giftocracy

noun, gif•toc•ra•cy: A system of governance in which our innate gifts are illuminated on the path to our purpose.

N ot too long ago, I heard Dr. Myles Munroe tell a powerful story that illustrates the essence of *Giftocracy*:

There once was a homeless man, sleeping on the street under a bridge, with an old cardboard box as his only shelter. Most days were spent hiding from the harsh reality and bitter cold of his existence. He begged for scraps and lived on others' charity. You could literally smell him from quite a distance.

One day, a fine gentleman in an exquisite limousine pulled up to a homeless camp and asked whether they knew a certain man he was seeking. "Yes," one of them replied. "He has been living with us on the streets for the past twenty-five years. He lives just a few blocks away from here." Joy filled the heart of the gentleman as he thought of uniting with that man. He quickly returned to his limousine and drove the few blocks in the direction the homeless man had pointed.

He soon found a group of men sitting together and walked over to them. Kneeling down in his fine suit, with little care as to the conditions he was in, he said the man's name, hoping that he was there. A man looked up from the group, squinting into the sun toward the voice. He looked so old—face and soul weathered by the hard life he'd lived—but he was barely forty-five.

"Do I know you?" he asked.

"No," replied the gentleman. "But I know you. I am your family—your uncle."

"I have no family," the man retorted. "I am alone in the world, and have been all my life."

"No," said the uncle. "I have come to bring you home."

"But this is my home," said the man.

"No, no. I want to take you *home*. I am all that is left of your family, but before your father passed away, he gave me something very special to give to you. I have searched far and wide and am so overjoyed to have found you! Please come home with me." The uncle pulled out a large envelope and held it out for the man. The man could not fully comprehend what the gentleman was saying and repeated that he had no family and that he belonged here, on the streets with his friends.

The uncle was greatly saddened as he looked at the surroundings and the poverty in which this man lived. He tried several more times to convince his nephew to come home, but the homeless man insisted he stay. He was happy here with his friends.

Finally, the uncle made one last plea: "I cannot force you to come back with me, but I will leave this envelope with you." As the uncle walked away, tears stained his eyes. He felt the loss like a weight tugging at his heart.

Strange as it seems, the homeless man cherished the envelope. He looked at it every day, relishing the fact that he was given a gift, a gift with *his* name on it. He would even show his friends this precious gift—but it remained unopened.

Many years later the homeless man died, still hugging the precious, unopened envelope. The envelope was taken off his body and handed over to an estate lawyer. Because the homeless man never opened the gift, he did not know that the envelope contained a deed to a multimillion-dollar estate and shares in the company his father had built. They were now all in his name. But since there was no one to claim ownership—the uncle had long since passed—the fortune was given to the state and it became government property. The homeless man had such an amazing future ahead of him, and such potential. But he died, never opening the gift.

This is a perfect illustration of our human condition. We are all born with tremendous gifts and potential, yet most people never "open" their gifts. Some do open their gifts for a time, but they lose touch with their potential as life beats them down and they experience adversity.

As a result, many people fail to connect with their passions and natural abilities, and consequently, their full potential is never realized. In essence, many people don't know who they really are. They don't know what they're capable of achieving. They never bothered to acknowledge a dream, much less chase it.

But it doesn't have to be this way. Life doesn't have to be an obstacle to merely overcome. When we wake up to a new day, we don't have to wonder how quickly we can get through it. We don't have to spend years—decades even—rehearsing the same questions in our minds: *Is this what I should be doing with my life? When will I finally be happy?*

My purpose in writing *Giftocracy* is not to help people appreciate that each human is a gift to the world (although they are), but to prove that each human *has* a gift trapped within, yearning to be experienced and shared.

Every human—no matter the country, century, or culture of birth—was born with his gift built into him. God, in His infinite wisdom, designed everything with its purpose already determined: A fish, for example, was created to swim. The ability and desire to swim is built into the fish. It never needs to attend swimming lessons. Similarly, a bird was created to fly. Flying is its nature. Likewise, a seed is planted in the ground with its future—a flower, a large oak tree, or a tomato vine—already inside of it.

Whatever we were created to be is already trapped inside of us, where we cannot miss it. The problem is that we spend our days looking everywhere else to find it.

One of the challenges we face (and the reason most people never discover their greatness) is because they are looking for their gift *outside of them*—in their environment. And think about how many people are stuck in the wrong environment? Environment is everything. Don't believe me? Think about the expression, "He's like a fish out of water." It means he's failing at whatever he's doing because he's been taken out of the only environment where he can succeed.

I have had the privilege of traveling extensively during my time as a professional soccer player, and later while coaching and working with youth. From the villages of Ghana to beautiful Santa Barbara, California, I have met people young and old who are desperately trying to find meaning and purpose but who don't know where to start.

I've seen young people who have been steered away from their unique gifts and encouraged by well-meaning people to follow a more traditional road. While a more traditional road may be popular, financially lucrative, or "acceptable" to our families, if the road does not embrace our gifts, the gift remains *unrealized*.

On the flip side, I have also witnessed the opposite. I've been in awe of people who have not only stepped into their gifts, but are also making an impact on our world every day. They have made it their mission to do good work that inspires others to do the same. Some of these people came from wealthy backgrounds, from families who encouraged them to use their gifts and succeed. Some of them came from poverty, from broken families, or from circumstances that provided little hope of a better life. What I'm saying is that purpose is not reserved for only the wealthy to discover.

When you are born in an environment of poverty where obtaining even the basics (like food and water) are a daily struggle, you find ways to distract yourself from your problems. Growing up in a small village in Ghana, my parents didn't have money to buy me lots of toys or videos games, but one day they did get me a soccer ball.

My first encounter with a soccer ball sparked something in me. I fell in love with it instantly and soon realized I was able to do things with a soccer ball that other children couldn't. Soccer came naturally to me.

When I played with the other kids in my village, everybody wanted me to be on their team because I was the best player. When I was dribbling a ball among ten other boys on a dirt field, that's when I felt like my most true self. Playing soccer, I was in an environment where I thrived—and I didn't want to be anywhere else.

When I played with my friends, I would often, without thinking, miss lunch and dinner. My parents had to come find me. In fact, my love of that environment got me into a lot of trouble at one point as a child! Still, I found my gift at an early age and was determined to use it, not knowing how far it would take me, but knowing I loved it and was willing to work at it. That determination took my mind off of my hungry stomach and trouble at home. Determination singularly refocused me from what was to what could be.

Even a child can develop the ability to overcome adversity when they are convinced they have found something that can make their lives significant. When you have a clear vision for your life, adversity simply becomes a test of your resolve—it cannot stop you. That's why visualizing dreams of the life we want is so important.

In my case, when I was living in my village in Odumaseh, Ghana, I dreamed that one day I would be traveling and playing soccer for European powerhouse Manchester United Football Club. Yes, it sounded impossible, looking at my circumstances. Yet that dream and vision literally guided my every decision—and it lead me across the world, right onto the soccer field for my first professional match against Manchester United.

This world is a challenging place to live, and I believe our vision has to be refreshed and refocused in order to add to its beauty. A Giftocracy is the place where our natural gifts merge with the things we do that bring us the most fulfillment. Can you imagine living in an environment where everyone loves Mondays, and everyone is sure that what he's doing is important? Giftocracy is a vision for that place.

Many popular self-help books say that to live your purpose, you have to look outside of yourself to get something that you don't already have, as if your future is far off, waiting to be found. But that's not the case at all. Your future is not outside of you—it is trapped *in* you, through the gifts you've been given.

Oftentimes, people think they need a major catalyst to find their purpose. They move to a new city, spend money they don't have, or chase degrees. But believe me, to start understanding your purpose, the only thing that needs a change is your mentality. More degrees, a change in location, the need to invest—those might follow, but, for now, start with the realization that you have a gift that resides in you. To truly live with purpose and fulfill that vision you may have labeled "impossible," you have to start unearthing your gift.

What if you don't know what your gift is?

Your gift is the single-most dominant thing you love to do, at your absolute best, with the least amount of effort. It is important for each of us to discover our gifts, not only because of the joy it will bring us, but also because our communities and nations need our gifts to bring hope, love, and justice to a world so desperately in need.

Giftocracy is not some nebulous, metaphysical, or philosophical ideology that works only in the distant future. Instead, it is people-ready and practical. It's not a religious dogma or some narrow philosophy that separates and segregates. And it's not just reserved for a special group of people. Giftocracy is first a pursuit of self. It is about discovering something that you *must* do, becoming passionate about what you were born to do.

It addresses the needs, wishes, aspirations, questions, and longings in the human experience, while exposing the defects, weaknesses, phoniness, and inferiority complexes inherent in our *own versions* of the truth. It is an idea for the rich, poor, child, and adult.

Giftocracy births your greatness, enlarges your leadership capacity, and gives life to others. If we are to become who we were created to be and live a purposeful life, we urgently need to embrace and change our perception of human potential—and we need to unwrap our gifts. This belief is part of my DNA, and my life is a testimony to it; this book is a hymn to the irrevocable power of our God-given gifts. May these pages help us capture that truth.

Join me on a journey of thought as we unwrap and unleash the gifts within us.

Are you ready?

PART ONE

Discovering the Gift:
The Purpose of Life is to
Discover Your Gift

CHAPTER ONE

MY STORY...AND WHY YOUR STORY MATTERS

"Never allow other people's opinions of you to
define your reality."

—Michael Tetteh

E veryone has a story—every life is a story. We are the sum
total of all those who have shaped our lives from birth. Our
lives begin with minimal understanding, requiring maximum
input from others. In just a few years, we reach the middle stage
of childhood when we begin adding our own processing and
intuition to the input of others. We process more intelligently
all thoughts of reality, both from our inner commands and
experience. Then we become adults, with our own sovereign will
and the responsibility to make choices. Somewhere along the
way, a strong feeling creeps into our minds: Are we truly living
the life we're intended to, or have we allowed the opinions of
others to shape who we are, leading us in a direction that was
never meant for us?

One day in particular is forever etched in my mind—the day I decided to never allow another person's opinions of me to shape who I was. I had just settled into Dunn School, a private high school in the hills of Santa Barbara, California. In a remarkable chain of events, I'd been given a full scholarship to attend school and play for the soccer team.

Just imagine yourself as a fifteen-year-old, thousands of miles away from home, in a strange city with a dream to play soccer professionally. The odds were in my favor, and I was excited to see what the future held for me.

My soccer coach from the academy in Ghana—the man who had chosen me out of five hundred children and who had become a role model and father figure—was visiting my high school and wanted to see how I was doing. After explaining to him that the desire to play professionally was burning in my heart, he looked at me like I was the biggest fool in the world. "You can't make it as a professional soccer player. You're not good enough. You played goalie growing up at the academy and won't be able to play any other position. Forget your dream of playing soccer professionally. You'd better focus on getting a degree so that you can get a good-paying job and make some money to help yourself and your family." His words were a crushing blow to everything I'd hoped for.

And just like that, the dream I'd held onto for so long hung in the balance.

For the Love of the Game

Growing up in Odumaseh, Ghana, my dream—even as a young boy—was to play professional soccer. In fact, when my mother was pregnant with me, she said I kicked my feet constantly—the first signs of a good soccer player. Gifted with speed, an intuitive understanding of the game, and endurance, I played soccer all day with my brothers and with other children in my village.

My soccer ball—made of rubber bands, plastic, and rope all tied together—was a constant companion. Chores like sweeping the dirt in front of our little house and washing the dishes of my elders were interrupted by brief juggling intervals. It seemed I was destined to play soccer. There was just one problem—to achieve my dream, I'd have to excel in school to win scholarships that would put me on the soccer field. And I *hated* school.

After a particularly rough day in math class, my parents grounded me. Not only that, they took away my soccer ball—the thing I loved most. For the next three weeks, I dressed in my school uniform so it looked like I was going to school, but as soon as I was far away from my house, I changed clothes and played soccer all day with friends.

While walking home one night, a friend told me the headmaster of my school had visited my parents because I'd missed so much school. Now that they knew I had been lying, I had two options: I could go home and confront them or run away. My nine-year-old mind chose the only sensible option—*run!*

That night was spent at a friend's house, and the next morning began my brief journey as a wandering child. For the next five days, I begged for food or offered to work for food or money. Some days I didn't eat or bathe. I slept on roadsides, in people's taxis, and under trees. I walked aimlessly for miles, missing my family, watching soccer matches along the way, and feeling like the world was against me.

One night, three men attacked me; they beat and kicked every part of my body and left me on the side of the road. Unable to move for hours, I cried and called for my parents. Alone and in pain, I realized what a terrible mistake I'd made. That night, I accepted responsibility for my actions, I regretted my behavior, and I was ready to face the consequences.

Although I was in immense pain, I finally decided to walk home—it seemed like twenty miles in the dark. The night was warm, and the air was filled with many different scents—some pleasing, some repelling. Not knowing how my parents would receive me, each step was filled with fear and hope. In what I can only call a remarkable showing of mercy, my parents welcomed me back with open arms. They told me, "Son, what you did was very bad, but we are glad that you came to that realization and are grateful for what you have. You learned an important lesson. You never know how good your life is or what you have until it is gone." My brief homelessness changed me.

No longer would the world owe me anything. Instead, it was I who owed the world. I was more determined than ever to use my gift—my love of soccer—for good. My attitude changed, and I developed an appreciation for the role of school and its importance.

Running after the Dream

The same night I returned home and apologized to my parents for running away, I heard on the radio that the very next day, there was going to be a soccer tryout for Right to Dream, which is an organization in Ghana that helps kids like me to achieve their dreams. The next morning, I ran two hours to the field to play with five hundred other kids who also came to try out, and then ran two hours back home after the first tryout. It was a weeklong tryout; every day, they cut the list down. After a week, eighteen children were selected. Thankfully, I was one of them. Training would begin immediately, and we were relocated to live with our coach at his team house.

My teenage years were spent at the academy. I was a very good goalkeeper and I was recruited by Dunn High School as a goalie.

When I got to my new high school in the US, I had a realization—at five-foot-eight, my height was always going to be questioned, since most of the college goalkeepers were at least six feet tall. Because the only way I could go to college was on a scholarship, I switched from a goalkeeper to a field player and began training with my friends every day.

Days started early. We would wake up at 5:00 a.m. before breakfast and go train. With my consistent work ethic and commitment, I slowly started getting better.

It may sound like an easy switch, but the transition wasn't without a great deal of effort. When you are a goalie, you are the last man standing: You can see the whole field, the big picture of the game, and can advise your defense or offense when he is out of position, or when he needs to drop back and defend. Because of this big-picture view, you develop good communication skills as a goalkeeper. But as a field player, you can't see the entire field at once. There was also the adjustment of being on a different part of the field and having different expectations that come with a new position.

I was laughed at by friends back home, and I was questioned by people whom I became friends with in the US. But I just believed in myself. I knew I could play on the field again, because when I was a little boy, I started playing as an outfield player and I was really good. I could do things with a soccer ball that most kids couldn't do. I had the speed, technical abilities, dribbling skills, and intuitiveness to see things on the field that most kids I grew up with couldn't see. Now, nearly a decade later, I concentrated on those original skills that enabled me to stand out as a little boy.

My high school soccer experience was great. Our team even took our high school to their first soccer championship! So when the harsh words of my visiting coach and mentor hung in the air between us—*You're not good enough*—I had an important choice to make. *Do I believe him and give up my dream? Or do I let his words fall to the ground like dirt and continue to pursue my dream?*

Sticks and Stones May Break My Bones, but Words...

Here I sat, across from this man whom I loved and respected. Very young and impressionable, I listened to his powerful words. He was the founder of the academy where I'd played for five years before coming to the US. My parents had been thrilled when I was chosen to play soccer, not only because it made me happy and took care of my needs, but also because it eased their burdens to provide for only four children instead of five.

In my time at the academy, he'd become more than a coach—he was a role model, a father figure, and an authority in our young lives. I remembered hearing his spirited cries of triumph as I kept the other teams from scoring, and his pride—his approval—reverberated in my young heart. As his athletes, we never questioned him. We feared him, and we put him on a pedestal.

But the fact that I had moved to Santa Barbara, California, to attend a private high school on a full scholarship, seemed not to play a role in this man's opinion of what my future could hold. "If I wasn't good enough, then how did I get here?" I asked myself.

> **Has anyone ever told you that, *in their opinion*, you couldn't become something? Have you ever listened to that person and let that person's *opinion* change your path, impact your sense of self, or complicate the relationship you have with your own personal destiny?**

I looked up and told him I believed I could make it to the pros. Without another thought, he said, "If that's the dream you want to pursue, then you're on your own." He didn't believe in me or in my dream. He never called me again to find out how I was doing.

I am not sure if my coach realized the impact he had on me that day. The funny thing is that I think he may have thought he was doing me a favor. Turning away from a man I once could have called my father, I realized this man was really a stranger.

Dreams dashed, I walked back to my dormitory in deep reflection. In the midst of all my sadness and anger, ancient wisdom came to mind: "As a man thinks in his heart, so is he."[1] I was instantly thankful to have spent a great deal of time reading the Bible. Perhaps it had prepared me for this moment. I also suddenly understood that in life, it's not what people say about you that matters. What matters is what you think and believe *about yourself.*

This was one man's opinion and nothing more. Who I was inside was still standing, still walking, and still deliberately moving toward my destiny, whether that meant soccer or not. I had come so far, and I chose not to let his words sink deep into my soul. I would not give up.

Digging Deep

What made me not give up after the whole conversation with my coach was simply my faith, my gift, and my past experiences. I had already gone through a lot in my youthful years, and all those experiences built within me a confidence that I would achieve something great in life.

After that conversation, I worked with extra diligence. I dedicated myself every day to training, running, and improving my soccer game.

> Have you ever had a role model give up on *your* dream? If so, realize it isn't *their* dream to give up on. You still have your dream!

I joined a local club team in Santa Barbara, California, called Legends. Also, while in high school, I traveled every summer with a soccer clinic called One Premier Soccer Schools. My soccer skills and technical abilities improved tremendously.

That hard work paid off, because, in my junior year of high school, I got letters from eight schools in California wanting me to sign with them. I eventually signed on with UCSB: University of California, Santa Barbara, with another full-ride scholarship to play soccer before twenty thousand fans.

Neither my academy director nor I knew exactly what my future held. But what I *did* know was that I was not willing to give up on my dream, nor let another person's opinion determine my destiny. Had I given up that day and allowed the words of my coach to penetrate my soul and become my reality, I would never have become one of the top-ranked college players, received a contract from Generation Adidas with Major League Soccer (MLS), and had my dream—of playing on the same field as the world-famous Manchester United—come true.

Stepping onto the Field of Dreams

It was July, and the weather was perfect for soccer. At age twenty-two, I had just been drafted by the Seattle Sounders Football Club in Major League Soccer (MLS). My dream had come true—I was a professional soccer player.

Every summer, top professional soccer teams from around the world came to the US for their preseason training games with the MLS teams. On this very day, it was going to be the sea of green mixed in with a sprinkle of red for the visitors— Manchester United. Nearly sixty-seven thousand diehard fans filled the stands, ready to cheer on their favorite team. What a day that was!

My childhood dream to play Manchester United was about to be fulfilled in a most spectacular way. You see, I grew up supporting Manchester United and considered myself a diehard fan. I spent the little money I had for food to buy clothing, socks, and every Manchester United accessory I could find. I had posters of the players on my wall and I would go to sleep at night with a Manchester United soccer ball, dreaming that one day I would get the opportunity to play alongside them. Now here I was, standing on the sidelines against the team I had idolized since I had been a child. It was surreal.

I went onto the pitch as a left back in the 64th minute and found myself under attack from Gabriel Obertan, a speedy Frenchman who was set to replace Cristiano Ronaldo and was trying to justify the five-million-dollar transfer fee that United had paid to acquire him. The game did not go well for us, and we yielded seven goals to zero in ninety minutes. Even though that game was one of the worst performances of my soccer career, the only thing going through my mind was that my childhood dream of playing on the same field as the team I once idolized had been fulfilled.

After the game, when the stadium was empty, I walked back onto the field to allow myself to fully absorb what had just happened. As I stood there in awe and gratitude, the words came rushing to my mind, and that still small voice reminded me: "A man's gift makes room for him in the world and brings him before great men."[1] Indeed, my gift made my dream possible that night—a dream backed up by thousands of hours of practicing, studying, and increasing my ability.

The World Needs Your Story

I want to give you a word of encouragement: Trapped inside you is a gift that will empower you to fulfill your vision and dreams. You were designed to be known for your gift, and, no matter how big the world is, there's a place for you in it. Your uniqueness and value in life is a product of your gift. No one can take it away. You can't be fired from it.

Whatever your dream, vision, or goal is, say with conviction to yourself: *My dream is possible!* It is your responsibility to use it to make the world a better place.

It's important to understand that we are all not gifted with the same talents and strengths, but each one of us has been created for a particular purpose and assignment. It is that gift that distinguishes you and sets you apart to fulfill your assignment on earth.

Never allow other people's opinions of you to define your reality.

Many times we become jealous of others by comparing ourselves to them, sometimes even comparing our weaknesses to their strengths! We look at their rewards to prove how we have missed our mark or to show we are not gifted. Yet, that's not true.

The uniqueness of your gift cannot be duplicated, though others might try to imitate it. This understanding then makes you responsible for the gift within you. You are responsible to express it, to release it, to nurture it, to develop it, to enhance it, and to bring it into the light.

How to Know Your Gift

The question we need to be asking ourselves is, how do we begin to understand our purpose? When the question of purpose becomes an esoteric, mystical concept that you cannot touch, smell, or hear, it feels elusive. It's nebulous and indefinable.

Purpose may not be tangible, but, like any good mystery, it leaves some clues to illuminate our path.

First, it's imperative that we come to the understanding that we are, indeed, gifted. Inside of you is a gift. It's not outside of you. It's not something you go out looking for. It's already trapped inside of you. Whatever your gifting is, you actually see the world through the lens of your gifting. The following indicators may also provide some clarity about your gift:

Indicator 1. You may be critical of others who are not gifted in that domain.

One of the best ways I have discovered in deciphering what a person's gift is, is that they tend to judge or be critical of others who are not gifted in that domain. I know this to be a fact because when I was a little boy growing up in Ghana, I knew that I was born with the gift of soccer. When I'm playing with others or watching other people play, I can quickly tell who has it and who doesn't. That is one of the best indicators of what your gift is.

Indicator 2. What do you find the most success in with the least amount of effort?

What talents or actions come naturally to you? What can you do at your maximum best, and yet it still doesn't feel like work?

Indicator 3. What problems do you like to solve?

Do you find yourself gravitating toward a particular problem in the world? Our world is filled with problems, and these problems give you the ability to use your gift. You and I were born to be problem solvers in the domain of our gifting.

When a young friend of mine was eleven years old, a bad relaxing-perm caused her hair to fall out. She was frustrated and embarrassed due to the traumatic experience. Her hair was damaged, breaking badly, and she could not find any all-natural alternatives for hair care. She vowed never to use harsh chemicals on her hair again and began conducting online research on how to create her own hair products using all-natural ingredients. She was determined to be a problem-solver.

She worked tirelessly until she discovered her Eden. It took nearly a year to create a new formula but she did and named herself as the CEO and founder of EDEN Body Works. Three years later, during an interview with Oprah, the TV icon asked her, "What made you think, 'I'll make my own'?" My friend smiled and responded, "I figured if it's not out there, do it for yourself."

Today, companies such as Wal-Mart, HEB, Walgreens, CVS, Target, Sally Beauty Supply, and Kroger sell her products. And EDEN BodyWorks—a vision that began in a basement in New Jersey—is estimated to be worth two million dollars.

For many people, that accomplishment would be more than enough. But my young friend had another vision. "Ever since I was eight years old, I knew I wanted to work in the field of robotics," she explained in a follow-up interview with Oprah.[1] She continued to run her hair-care business while attending Georgia Tech, where she graduated with a degree in computer science. She now serves as a project manager on the XBOX ONE engineering team.

While her workweek is spent at Microsoft, any free time is spent giving interviews, designing new labels and products, and traveling to speak at different conferences and events. In addition, she's pursuing her Masters of

Science in Human Centered Design and Engineering at the University of Washington. "Pursuing my Masters degree and working two jobs…some people might think I'm crazy, but I like to say that I'm very motivated."

My young friend is worth millions of dollars but most importantly, she's creating solutions that help people solve their problems.

When you study people's problems, understand their problems, and can provide a solution to the problems, they will invite you into their life and they will reward you financially.

Take time to study the problems of your world. Whether it's the world of entertainment, finance, beauty, business, education, sports, or politics, these domains all have problems to be solved. When problems arise, your gift comes alive! You were not born to simply make a living. You were born to make a difference and to influence your generation—which you can do by using your gift to solve problems within a particular domain.

I Just Graduated…Now What?

Many recent graduates are trying to figure out what they want to do with their lives. And to be honest, there are plenty of forty-, fifty-, and sixty-year-olds who are asking that very same question.

Career decisions become critical: One decision can lead you into a career that pays your bills but leaves you miserable. Unfortunately, many people are living to pay bills instead of living to make a difference.

Some people will tell recent graduates to "just get a job and figure it out." I, however, would give this advice to all young people who are considering career moves: Find out first what your gift is. Just like Jasmine demonstrated with her determination to create products that help others, find your gift and go do that (or at least something that allows you to fully use your talents), because doing anything else will frustrate you.

Your gift is the thing that you love to do at your absolute best with the least amount of effort.
—Steve Harvey

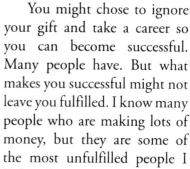

You might chose to ignore your gift and take a career so you can become successful. Many people have. But what makes you successful might not leave you fulfilled. I know many people who are making lots of money, but they are some of the most unfulfilled people I have ever met. Their lives are filled with stress, worry, and all kinds of challenges. In fact, I actually believe that it is possible to be successfully wrong. Why? Because you are succeeding in something that you were never born to do.

Tiger Woods, LeBron James, Michael Jordan—these guys have a gift, and when you watch them, it's written all over them. Your gift may be soccer, comedy, accounting, teaching, or music. Whatever your gift, when you become aware of it and as you strengthen it, opportunities will appear that you couldn't have predicted. The key is—*you* have to do the legwork.

Many people are waiting for something or someone to pull them through, pull them up, or give them a hand. We gravitate toward people who are striving to become successful, and we develop a mentality that says, "When they get there, they will make room for us." But when it doesn't happen, we shift responsibility to someone or something else. That's what I call the spirit of irresponsibility. While it's certainly kind to help others reach the next level or to be helped yourself, we shouldn't *depend* on it.

We've developed the attitude that *people owe us something.* We will wait for assistance for years and years without taking the first step on our own. Often, we feel like no one is there for us, helping us. Yet, your gift isn't about them. Your gift is your own to unwrap and nurture. Only then can you share it with others.

It Starts with a Seed

Every human being came to earth with a gift. God never told Adam to be *seedful*. His first command to mankind was to be *fruitful*—to be productive. Yet, it's impossible to be fruitful unless you have a seed. Fruit is a product of a seed. Your gift is the seed placed inside of you that's meant to produce something for your generation.

When you put an apple seed in the right environment, just that one apple seed will produce countless apples. Over time, it can produce an entire apple orchard. The seed is loaded, but all you and I see at the start is that one little seed. It's the same with your gift. Your gift is like a seed that's waiting to produce—it's loaded with potential.

The world won't move over for you just because you're smart and have the right education, experience, or connections. However, when you exercise your gift, not only will the world make room for you, but it will also pay you for your gift! Anyone—yourself included—who discovers his gift and nurtures, develops, and enhances it will become a sought-after commodity.

If you're a young person in high school or college who is planning your career, don't do what people say will make you a lot of money. Do what you were born to do, because that is where you will make your money. No matter how big the world is, there's a place for you in it when you discover and manifest your gift.

In the biblical story of David and Goliath, we must understand that it was David's gift that made room for him and brought him before great men. It was not his education, nor the people he knew, but his gift, and the fact that he had spent years practicing it. David's gift brought him from the shepherd's dump to the front of the palace, where he became the captain of Saul's military base. No one remembers his brothers, who thought he was crazy. We only remember the boy who believed he could kill Goliath.

Just like David, you become valuable based on the problems you solve. My spiritual father Myles Munroe says, "Never ask God to remove every Goliath you meet. Stop praying for deliverance from your success." When the problems show up in your life—and they will—don't ask God to remove them because problems are simply an opportunity to learn about yourself. If there had been no Goliath, there would never have been a King David. That giant Goliath was his ticket to greatness!

Stop trying to run away from your greatness. The problems you're facing have been sent to give you value. And your value goes up when you solve problems. Instead of running from problems in your job, marriage, or business, face them and embrace them because those problems will introduce you to your greatness.

You are never remembered for the things you avoided. You're remembered for the things you survived.
—Myles Munroe

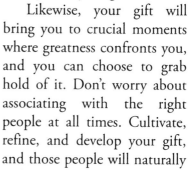

Likewise, your gift will bring you to crucial moments where greatness confronts you, and you can choose to grab hold of it. Don't worry about associating with the right people at all times. Cultivate, refine, and develop your gift, and those people will naturally find their way to you. The better refined your gift, the farther it will take you in life.

If your desire is to coast along, doing things halfway, chances are you'll find a job. But you should know you will, in that case, be simply an employee. However, if you decide that you're going to find the calling that is truly yours, then you will fulfill your vision and you will be remembered by others.

On that magical day on the soccer field, playing against a team I had long dreamed of, I saw a fulfillment of the words of a very wise man: "A man's gift makes room for him and brings him before great men."[2] What brought me from a tiny mud hut in Ghana to playing professional soccer was my gift. My gift was the vehicle that transported my life to many parts of the world.

Yes, it's important that you have people in your life who love you and support you, but know that what will make room for you in the world is not the connections you have; it's your gift that will ultimately open doors.

What I love about Solomon's statement above regarding how a man's gift makes room for him, is that it strips competition, conformity, compromise, and the comparison out of living. The day you finally meet yourself, you will be stripped of all these. The truth is, when you discover your gift, you automatically know that nobody is going to be better at it than you. You are never going to be better than me at being me, and I am never going to be better than you at being you. As unique and great as I am in my domain, so too are you unique and great in your domain. If everybody discovered his domain of gifting, there would be no more competition or comparison—only camaraderie.

I know what it feels like to doubt or to feel as though you have nothing. But I'm here to tell you that everybody has something—some great purpose. Deposited in you is a unique gift—a dream that yearns to be fulfilled.

"Aedh Wishes for the Cloths of Heaven"
by William Butler Yeats

Had I the heavens' embroidered cloths,
Enwrought with golden and silver light,
The blue and the dim and the dark cloths
Of night and light and the half-light,
I would spread the cloths under your feet:

But I, being poor, have only my dreams;
I have spread my dreams under your feet;
Tread softly because you tread on my dreams.

Every day and everywhere, both children and adults spread their dreams, their gifts, and their talents beneath our feet. With one single word, we can lift them up or dash their hopes. Especially when it comes to children, we must tread softly and not squash the dreams our children have deep in their hearts. We must encourage them and support them, no matter how unreasonable and outlandish their dreams might be. We must create the right environment for their dreams to be fulfilled.

May we all be willing to see the dreams inside our children's hearts and to nurture the gifts within. When the seed is watered, it will grow.

CHAPTER TWO

THE GENESIS OF THE GIFT

"The value in each human is the gift they were born
to deliver to humanity."
—Myles Munroe

The key to understanding your gift and your purpose on
earth is to first understand the original intent for humanity
in general. When we know God's intentions from the very
beginning, then we can understand who we truly are and how we
fit into His plans. This gives us a better context—the big picture.
And since God is a God of purpose, everything He does has a
calculated purpose and a plan.

Every manufacturer that creates a product first starts with
purpose, then moves on to production. *Purpose* here is defined
as "intent." If we fail to discern intent, abuse or ignorance will
follow. I believe this is the reason our world is confused, with so
many people living meaningless lives. Because we haven't properly
understood God's original intent, we have also misunderstood
not only ourselves but also this beautiful planet we call earth. If
we fail to know what our original intent is, then everything we do
and continue to do will be a waste of our potential.

On the Seattle Sounders Soccer Club, during training sessions, our assistant coach would always emphasize that we needed to see the whole field. He would say, "Put yourself in a position on the field so you can see everything, see where each player is, and see the spaces on the field to pass the ball to. Don't narrow your vision of the field; otherwise, you will miss good scoring opportunities." If we only see or hear a small part of the bigger picture, we can't understand the full intent, and we will inevitably draw incorrect conclusions.

The Big Picture

Being a man of faith, I believe everything begins with the Creator. Whenever life's bigger lessons demand a more personal interpretation, I use the Bible—an important navigational tool—as a straightforward way of tracing life's meaning back to its origin. So what was God's original intent when He created you?

His original plan and purpose was to extend His invisible heavenly Kingdom to the visible earthly Kingdom. The strategy was for heaven to colonize earth. Therefore, humans were created as His sons and daughters to administrate that extension of His heavenly kingdom, and to colonize earth through a system He calls "dominion."

In colonization, the goal is to influence the new place with the culture from the original land, so that the people take on the values, standards, lifestyle, and culture of the colonizing kingdom. This is why you continue to see the influence of other cultures on countries today. This is true even if the colonized country has gained independence. When you study history, this is what many preexisting kingdoms tried to do, but failed because their intentions were evil.

When the British arrived in Ghana in the early 1820s, the average Ghanaian had never visited England, much less heard of the country; but, by watching the lifestyles of the Europeans in Ghana, my people learned what life was like in England, Portugal, and France. We watched the recreational habits of the British and noticed that, for fun, they'd kick a ball up and down a field and try to knock it between two goals—and they called it football, or soccer. We learned that, every afternoon, the British stopped whatever they were doing to have tea. In other words, without ever traveling to England, we learned what life was like there. When you travel to Ghana today, you'll see we drink tea, not coffee, because that's what British colonizers drank. We speak English, not French, because that was the language spoken in Britain. In other words, when a country or land is colonized, the culture of the colonizer is transferred to the existing culture.

But Jesus never taught us to pray so that we can go to heaven. His instructions were that we should pray for heaven to come to earth through our work. The great problem is that we are in a hurry to leave the earth and get our ticket to heaven. This is one of the biggest mistakes we have made in the church, and it's the very reason why most people ignore and never discover their gifts.

We have reversed the instructions and have preoccupied ourselves with teaching, training, and preparing people to *leave the earth*—when, in fact, God's instruction and intent is for us to *occupy the earth* by using our gifts to bring hope, love, and justice to a world so desperately in need (until He comes back). His original intent is for you and I to fill the earth with our Kingdom gift…creating a Giftocracy.

The Kingdom Concept: Dominion or Democracy?

I grew up in a very religious environment. As a little boy in Ghana, going to church wasn't an option—it was a requirement. Still, even in my teenage years, I heard very little in church about the Kingdom of God. I learned about grace, healing, prosperity, faith, and deliverance, but nothing on the message Jesus focused on so often—the Kingdom.

Years later, when I went to college at UCSB, I took a communications class. One of the first things I learned in that class was that when you want to communicate with someone, it is important to communicate in concepts. If I want to talk with you and make sure you understand what I'm sharing, I have to make sure that the concepts I have in my mind are the same in your mind. I have to convey my concept or idea clearly to you, because if our concepts don't match, that's called a *misconception*. Therefore, when the Bible uses terminology like *Kingdom*, the question we must first ask is, "What did Jesus mean?"

First, it's important to note that the Kingdom concept is completely opposite to a democracy or a republic. Jesus came preaching about a Kingdom, not a democracy. There is no democracy in the Bible. In a kingdom, there is no vote; but in democracy, the power is in the vote. In a democracy, you have a president or a prime minister; but in a kingdom, you have a king. In a democracy, you elect your leader; but in a kingdom, the king elects his citizens.

So why does all that matter? Take America, for example. The Constitution begins with "We the people." But in the Bible, God's Constitution for life begins with our King or Lord. In God's Kingdom, there's no such thing as a referendum or debate. We cannot change God's laws. We cannot improve on what He has done. That's why the Bible says, "But the word of the Lord endures forever."

Sadly, in the twenty-first century, religious Christianity has become a democracy. Yet this was never God's intention from the very beginning, and certainly not what Jesus intended. We were all sent to the earth to rule, lead, and govern the planet, and it's in our DNA to want to be in charge and in positions of leadership. In fact, God's original intent is emphatically stated in the early chapters of the Bible:

> Then God said, "Let us make man in our image, after our likeness. And let them have dominion over the fish of the sea and over the birds of the heavens and over the livestock and over all the earth and over every creeping thing that creeps on the earth."[3]

In this statement, we know why God created humans. We are told what to do in an area of our gifting. At the core of our very being is a spirit endowed and crowned with glory and honor, with authority over and management of the earth and the rest of creation—but never over other people. The key in life is to find your area of gifting. It is in the domain you are meant to dominate.

Every man and woman, boy and girl, was created to dominate a specific domain of life with his or her gifts. Therefore, the discovery of your gift is the discovery of your domain and of your personal purpose. When you find your gift, you become a person of purpose. The discovery of your purpose births your leadership.

A true leader is more focused on discovering himself than on controlling and manipulating people. If you discover your gift, master it, and dominate your area of gifting, people will be *attracted* to you. This is why I love this thought from Dr. Myles Munroe: "True leaders never seek followers. Followers are attracted to the gift of the leader."

With the big picture in mind, I want to share a story that changed my life—and I want you to understand why it's important for you to find your own gift as a human.

Understanding Potential

I was drafted by the Seattle Sounders soccer club, a professional soccer team in the US. During my time on the team, I became good friends with one of my teammates, Steve Zakuani, who gave me a book by his mentor, Dr. Myles Munroe. Dr. Munroe used a metaphor in his book, *Understand Your Potential*, that struck a deep chord in my heart and etched itself in my memory forever. He said, "The wealthiest spot on planet earth is not the gold mines of South America, the silver mines of Central America, the diamond mines of South Africa, the Uranium mines of Europe, or the oil fields of Iran, Iraq, and Saudi Arabia. The wealthiest place on earth is the cemetery." In an instant, I understood what he meant. This statement absolutely changed my life.

Why is the cemetery the wealthiest place on earth? Because buried in the graveyard are the gifts, talents, skills, leadership, solutions, abilities, ministries, businesses, and potential of people who never fully lived. In the cemetery, you will find books unwritten, songs unsung, poetry uncomposed, music never fully played, goals never scored, recipes never tasted, and businesses that never realized their first dollar. So often people take their awesome treasures to the graveyard. What a wealthy place! If we could mine the gifts and talents buried in the cemetery like we mine diamonds and gold, we would be very wealthy.

In Africa, for example, our natural resources are being mined and exploited for profit. Wars are fought over precious diamonds and gold, and many lives are lost in the pursuit of these treasures. My hope is that you will not take your treasure to the cemetery, because you have immense potential. We must understand the treasure of unlimited potential within us and commit to unlocking that treasure to humanity during our short existence on earth.

Potential Produces

So what is potential? In the book *Understanding Your Potential*, Myles Munroe describes it as dormant ability, untapped power, hidden strength, reserved power, kept capacity, unused success, and unleashed talent. Potential is all that you can do but haven't done yet; it's the totality of who you are, but it hasn't manifested yet. And it's always trapped on the inside.

Potential is God's way of letting us know that we can't settle for our past achievements, because there's still more left in us to achieve. The problem is that we can become so attracted to our current success that we stop moving toward our *next* success.

Nothing can stop you from growing faster than success. I have seen it happen so many times in soccer. During my college years, we won a big game in front of fifteen thousand people. After the game, we all went out to celebrate. Everybody was impressed with our performance because we had come into the game as the underdogs and we had won. But instead of us focusing on playing the next game, which was in three days, we went out partying. What happened at our next game? It was a disaster, and we lost badly.

How was that possible after playing so well three days earlier? Our level of talent hadn't changed—but our focus had. We were riding so high on our success that our focus on the next game switched off. Success is fantastic, but it should never allow you to believe you've peaked, blocking you from even achieving more success. You can become so proud of what you have already done that your pride prevents you from doing what you could do. As

Myles Munroe said, "The greatest enemy to your potential progress is your last success."

Celebrate what you have already done. Let it motivate you to tap more into your potential, but ask God to lead you to the next thing in your life. He never stops, and you cannot stop either.

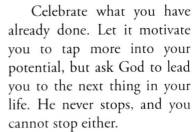

> You can become so proud of what you have already done that it prevents you from doing what you could do.[4]

The Seed Principle

The Creator does nothing without potential, because He built potential into everything He created. To simplify the concept of potential within the context of our gifts, I want to show you one of the most powerful elements in nature—the *seed*. Like a seed, your purpose lies inside you, and when it comes out, you can see its fruit. Isn't it amazing that when you pluck fruit from a mango tree or an apple tree, it keeps producing? The apple tree doesn't stop producing because you pick one apple from it. New fruit grows in its place.

Let's consider some powerful statements from the book of Genesis that afford us the knowledge and understanding of our gifts. Genesis 1:11–12 are two of my favorite verses in the Bible. God created the universe, created our planets, created our solar system, created the earth, and then started creating life on the earth. In Genesis 1:11, God revealed to us how everything is made:

> Then God said, "Let the land produce vegetation: seed-bearing plants and trees on the land that bear fruit with seed in it, according to their various kinds." And it was so.

The land produced vegetation; plants bearing seed according to their kinds and trees bearing fruit with seed in it according to their kinds. And God saw that it was good."

Many times, with modern translations of the Bible, we don't really understand the gravity of what we are reading. The Bible was written in Hebrew, not English. In the original Hebrew language, here's how the verse is written (with my emphasis):

And the Lord God made trees, and the plants and He hid in them their own seeds and *God placed the seed of everything in itself.*

In other words, everything that God created, He created with potential inside. The future of a seed can't happen ahead of the seed—the future of the seed is *trapped inside* the seed.

For instance, if I have an apple seed in my hand right now, it looks like a plain old seed. That's a fact, but it's not the whole truth. A fact is defined as a description of the present state of things. Truth is defined as the true reality of a thing. In this case, the truth would be that I have an entire apple tree in my hand because the potential of one seed to grow into a giant apple tree is there. But to say that there's only one apple tree trapped inside limits its potential. In fact, because of how each apple on that tree contains seeds, there are millions of possible apple trees that originate from that one seed. When you hold a seed in your hand, what you are holding is the potential of an apple orchard. That's the "Seed Principle."

When you kill a seed, you're not killing a seed—you're destroying an orchard. It's the same principle in our own lives. There's a great man in every little boy. There's a powerful woman in every little girl. This is why we can never ignore or devalue anyone. We simply don't know what potential is hidden inside, waiting to be brought out. Think about those people you went to high school or college with who've gone on to make an incredible mark on this world, though you never saw it coming. Don't give up on anyone. Ever.

My question to you is this: Have you found your seed? What are the characteristics of your seed? Is it an apple seed, a grass seed, or a cilantro seed? Whatever type of seed you are carrying, you must first know how to take care of it properly so that it can produce fruit or grass or herbs.

You were designed by the Creator to deliver a seed to your generation, just like the statement in Proverbs: "A man's gift makes room for him in the world and brings him before great men." No matter how crowded the world may seem, your seed is your God-given gift. And the world needs it. At this very moment, seven billion people occupy this planet. Your gift and the experiences you've accumulated differentiate you from the other 6,999,999,999 people alive today.

The fact that you were born is proof that you are supposed to uniquely contribute something to this world. No human being ever came to earth without a purpose. As I like to say, no one came here empty. When you exercise your gift, you're doing what God wants you to do on earth.

Be Fruitful and Multiply

After God created the seed in Genesis 1:11–12, His next statement to all the created things was to be fruitful and multiply:

God blessed them and said, "Be fruitful and multiply in number and fill the waters in the seas, and let the birds multiply on the earth."

Each creature that God created (including everything that lives on the ground, in the water, or in the air) must be fruitful. God never said to be "seedful." He never said to keep your gift under lock and key, only to be used on special occasions, like fine china. He said to be fruitful. The word *fruitful* here means to be productive. God's first command to you is to be *productive*—to produce something. If He commands you to do it, then it must mean that it's in your power to do, because it wouldn't be fair for Him to ask you to do something that you're not equipped to do. Just as you'll only learn how strong your body is if you regularly exercise it, so it goes with your gift.

More than One Gift?

Though everyone is born with at least one gift, sometimes we are given supplementary gifts. When I was growing up, I was aware of the two giftings that God gave me—soccer and teaching. Both were meant to help me fulfill my purpose, my assignment on the earth. It was my gift of soccer (that came alive when I was growing up) that gave me opportunities that led to where I am today. But my gift of teaching was just as important.

When I was at the academy, I was the one gathering all of my teammates together once a week to teach them biblical principles. This teaching, mentoring, and encouraging others came naturally to me. I could (and still can) take a scripture in the Bible and easily apply it to life. In fact, many pastors have said that I am meant to be preaching or pastoring a church.

When I was told to let go of soccer (the game that I loved so much), I wasn't being asked to give up a gift or let it die; I was simply moving from one gift to another. I would move from scoring goals for men with my gift of soccer, to scoring goals for the Kingdom.

Puzzle Pieces

Oftentimes, the questions surrounding our gifts seem so esoteric, imprecise. In order to understand the ideas of gifting and purpose in practical terms, I used my car as a teaching tool. After I'd bought an Audi, I took it back to the dealership and asked the mechanic to explain to me how the engine of my car worked. The mechanic that day was a wonderful gentleman. He took me outside, opened my car, and began to explain to me in detail how the engine functions. While he was talking, I was taking notes and studying the engine.

He said to me, "Michael, in the engine of any car are many components, or parts that make up the engine of a car that perform a specific function." He went on to say that each component that makes up the engine is designed to serve or contribute to a purpose and if it's not providing a service, it shouldn't be there. It became very evident to me that the manufacturer, who designed the engine of my car, designed each component of the engine to serve a function—a specific purpose for the successful operation of the vehicle. Each component of the engine is significant, necessary, unique, and important—just like us!

The relationship between a manufacturer and its product fascinated me. The engine was like a big puzzle. Each piece was necessary to form the whole and to ensure that it ran well. Looking at humanity, I can easily imagine we are pieces in a great puzzle, components on a vast planet, part of something bigger than ourselves. We are a significant and integral part of creation, specially engineered to serve in some capacity. If we are not able to add value to humanity, we will feel incomplete because we were created to serve, to add value. There is a gift inside of us that is meant to be deployed in service to others.

Followers and Leaders

When we think of leadership, we think that we need to have followers before we can be leaders. And so we preoccupy ourselves with trying to find followers. In the process, we lose sight of what true leadership is all about. A true leader is not the one who has and maintains followers. A true leader is the one who produces *more leaders*. True leaders don't seek followers. Followers are actually attracted to the gift of the leader. When followers become your pursuit as a leader, you are doomed for failure. Leadership has more to do with self-discovery than with seeking followers.

When I say that everyone was born to lead, your first reaction might be this: "If everyone is supposed to rule and lead, who is going to follow?" Remember when I said earlier that we are created to rule over our dominion, but not over other people? This is one of the most difficult concepts for us to understand, but also one of the most important. Our culture tells us that to be a ruler, to be great, or to be a leader, you need followers. But that simply isn't true. In fact, the Chinese have a proverb that enforces this misconception about rulership and leadership. They say, "He who thinketh he leadeth and has no one following him is only taking a walk."

Throughout history, every person who became a great ruler or leader never sought followers. They gained followers by operating in their gifts, much like a tree draws people and animals to it in order to eat the fruit. When you have fruit, people will seek you out and tell others about you.

When I was a young boy in Ghana, there was a man living about ten blocks from our village who had many mango trees in his yard. Many times, when my parents couldn't provide food for us, I remember walking with my friends to the fence that seemed five times taller than us. Our hunger and desire for those mangoes was stronger than our fear of the fence. Suddenly, we realized that we could climb the fence, and we found ourselves on the other side, stealing his mangoes so we could eat that day. Even his dogs weren't a deterrent!

When people see your fruit, they will leap over others and any obstacle in their way to get to you. When you develop and refine your gift, they will find you. But first, you have to find your gift before you can refine it. When your gift is discovered, that's when your true leadership is birthed.

What Makes a Person a Success?

You become successful by becoming a man or a woman of value. When you become valuable, people pay you to be yourself. That's why a person who is truly great is never proud, doesn't seek money, and doesn't seek relationships. They are busy being themselves, and that's why people want to be with them; we love to be near authenticity. I am never attracted to fake people and you're likely not either. We can usually tell when someone is operating under false pretenses, personal agendas, or with ill intents. These people may have success for a while, but they cannot sustain it if they are using their gifts for only self-serving purposes. When you know who you are, and use it for the good of others, that makes you a success.

People will always be attracted to your gift, but not necessarily to *you*. Thankfully, I understood this truth at an early age. When I was playing soccer, I understood why agents were calling, and why coaches were coming after me. They were coming after my gift because they knew that my gift could help their team. Yes, in a way, this can feel like you're being used for your gift, and some people are more gracious than others when presenting you with opportunities where your gift will be utilized. But we must remember that our gift is meant to be shared with others. This understanding can help protect you from being disappointed by rejection or missed opportunities.

A person who is a true leader and who manifests their greatness never does it for the approval of people. They do it just because that's who they are. In the end, it's about them committing themselves to serving people, no matter what, with dignity.

CHAPTER THREE

EDEN: ENVIRONMENT MATTERS

"The first step toward success is taken when you
refuse to be a captive of the environment you first
find yourself in."

—Mark Caine

As a boy, I used to help my grandfather with his corn farm as well as other farmers in our village. Early on, I noticed something about farming—farmers never make seeds grow. Farmers simply create the environment that the seed needs to bring out the fruit trapped in it. Similarly, when you discover your gift, the environment you are in will determine whether the world sees your gift or not; your environment can even determine the growth—or stagnation—of your gift.

The ability to share our gifts is determined by our ability to find those environments that are most conducive to sharing. In some cases, that means abandoning places that drain us of our purpose. We must be willing to examine and analyze our environment. Is our environment positive or negative? Uplifting or degrading? Does it enrich us spiritually, mentally, and physically? Does our environment enhance or ignore the presence of a Creator?

Environment is the key to life. Without the right environment, our gifts are at risk of not achieving their full potential. We must agree to never stay in any environment that doesn't develop, refine, enhance, or nurture our gift.

Creating Your Ideal Environment

Everything in life is meant to live in a specific environment, so that it can function how the manufacturer promised it would. This is why when you buy any man-made products, there's a list of dos and don'ts regarding use. There's also a guide to where products should and *shouldn't be* used. If you violate the environment that the manufacturer established, the product won't function properly or maximize its full potential. In some cases, using the product in the wrong environment can destroy the product entirely or cause great harm to you, the user.

We're used to these warnings on products like hairdryers, TVs, and coffeemakers, but the same laws apply to animals and plants. All living creatures must obey the irrefutable laws of order that govern the earth if they are to unlock the potential trapped in them and fulfill their calling.

Fish, plants, stars, and humans were all designed to live in a specific environment:

- A fish's environment is the ocean.
- A plant's environment is the soil.
- A star's environment is the galaxy.
- A human's environment is the presence of God.

If a fish is out of its environment, it will die. If a star is out of its environment, it becomes a meteorite and burns up. If a man or woman is out of the presence of God, they suffer from a loss of connection to their Creator. Every created thing has an ideal environment.

Merriam-Webster dictionary gives us two important definitions of *environment* that I want to draw your attention to:

a. the conditions and influences that affect the growth, health, progress, etc., of someone or something

b. the circumstances, objects, or conditions by which one is surrounded

God designed everything to function within a specific environment. This suitable makeup—designed, by God, for each created thing to function—is the place we call environment. As the environment was prepared, God called and placed each thing in its intended environment for growth, health, and progress to take place.

In Genesis, we find these statements:

Let the waters under the heavens be gathered together into one place, and let the dry land appear. And it was so. God called the dry land earth and the waters that were gathered together He called seas. And God saw that it was good. Let the earth sprout vegetation, plants yielding seed, and fruit trees bearing fruit in which is their seed, each according to its kind, on the earth. And it was so." (See Genesis 1:9–11.)

In other words, only when the environment was ready did God speak His handiwork into being, commanding it to bring forth its potential. Before He created plants, land animals, and sea animals, He made sure the environment for each creature had been prepared. He gathered the waters together so that the dry ground would appear before He spoke plants, land animals, and sea animals into being. If He took this much care in creating the right environment for animals and plants, why wouldn't He do the same for us?

This law of environment is not only restricted to God—everyone who creates a product also uses the same process. For example, when I signed my first professional contract, one of the benefits was that the league gave all signed players a stipend to buy furniture and other items for our homes. When I received mine, the first thing I bought was a big flat-screen TV and a surround-sound system so I could watch soccer games.

To set the TV up, I opened the manual that came with the product and one of the first things I read said, "Please read this manual carefully, as it contains valuable information about the product that will help you maximize the full enjoyment of it." The manual said, "Do not operate the TV near water." Now, if I took the television and tossed it into the ocean near our house, and tried to make it work, the obvious answer would be that it would not. This action would ruin the product because I would have placed the TV in the wrong environment. So when any product starts to operate outside of its intended environment, the product will not work—including humans. Knowingly being in the wrong environment means you're allowing the abuse of your potential.

Just as there are plenty of wrong environments for products, there's an ideal environment for the maximum performance of that product. An ideal environment includes the perfect conditions and influences that affect growth, health, and success. This is precisely why God, the great Architect and Manufacturer of humans, created a specific environment called Eden so that humans could understand, release, and maximize all that He placed in them. Eden, therefore, is our ideal environment.

Eden: Your Ideal Place to Be

When God, in His infinite wisdom, was creating His apex of creation, He didn't just put humans anywhere. He had a specific place in which humans would function at their peak performance. God didn't only plan what men would be (spirit) and how they would function (faith), but He also established the place where humans would live (Eden).

The etymology of the Hebrew word *Eden* is unclear, but we do know the Greek version of the Old Testament relates to the Hebrew verb *eden*, or *aden*, which means "delight or pleasure."[5] So Eden is the garden of delight. It was a pleasant garden environment—a place filled with pleasure, love, and beauty—a place where God's presence dwelt. Eden was a place on the earth where God's presence was literally tangible to humanity.

> **God's delightful presence is human's ideal environment.**

Eden was an open door between God and man! So when Adam was created, God put him in Eden and filled it with His presence, and Adam walked and talked with God in the cool of the day. This is why, in Genesis 1 and 2, Adam didn't have to pray or do any of the things most Christians do today. He did not have access to universities or any other system of obtaining knowledge. Adam had direct access to God, and whatever God wanted him to do, God communicated it through his soul and Adam manifested it on the physical planet.

You may say, "Well, that sounds great, but Eden doesn't exist anymore. So how can I function at my best if there's no such thing as an ideal environment anymore?" To that I say, think again!

Yes, the Garden of Eden was a physical place where God walked and talked with Adam and Eve. After The Fall, Adam and Eve were banished from the garden and separated from their special relationship with God. But for us today, Eden is not just a place that once was; it's an encouraging and nourishing environment—even a frame of mind. Even though the totality of the true Eden will be fully restored when Jesus comes back again, He has restored it, in part, through Jesus's death. In other words, Eden is any environment that's conducive to the growth of our gifts. You can bring Eden back into your home, your friendships, and anything that you do.

Is Your Environment Positive or Negative?

Now that we know what ideal environment we should live in, it's time to do some soul-searching to see if we're actually living in an atmosphere that will allow us to fulfill our gift. Think about your daily environment: Does it enrich you spiritually, mentally, and physically? Is it uplifting or degrading? Does it challenge you to be a better individual daily or does it remove you from the presence of God?

Here's a checklist of environmental conditions to consider:

- Who are your friends?
- What books do you read?
- What movies do you watch?
- What magazines fill your shelves?
- What are your hobbies?
- What are your recreational activities?
- Who feeds your musical appetites?
- Who are your heroes?
- Who feeds you spiritually?
- Are the conditions of your home, school, work, or play conducive to your goals in life?

Have you ever noticed how beautiful and efficient fish are in the water, or how beautiful birds are when they are flying in the sky, or how amazing it is that plants can grow in the right type of soil? A fish in water, just like a bird in the air, is majestic, powerful, beautiful, and awe-inspiring. Yet, take a fish out of the water, and what do you have? You have a creature that, instead of generating power, generates your sympathy, looks pathetic, flops around helplessly, and cannot survive. If we're being honest, we can think of at least one person who fits this description. Maybe we've even been there ourselves—hopeless, and seemingly unable to survive in our current situation.

Many are stuck in careers, vocations, and jobs where they don't belong and can't seem to find fulfillment. If you're in the wrong environment—whether that's a job, a relationship, a community, or a mind-set—there is sometimes nothing you can do to make you fit in there if you truly don't belong. Maybe you've simply outgrown your current environment. Or maybe you were never meant to stay there in the first place.

Maybe there is something bigger in your mind and heart than that little cube they have boxed you in, the stereotype others have given you, or the titles passed on to you by family and friends. Until you discover your gift, you will never see how beautiful, glorious, majestic, and competent you are.

We need seven billion people on earth to each discover his own domain instead of trying to be like everyone else. Your gift is your vehicle, your ticket, your plane, your car, your opportunity, your freedom, your option. It's what will destroy the obstacles you face, and what will bring you before the domain of excellence and greatness.

To manifest your greatness, your gift requires the right environment. Even if you have to distance yourself for a time from your mother, father, family members, education system, job environments, or friends, surround yourself with people who believe in you and your dream. Don't keep company with dream-killers and vision-destroyers who tell you that you can't make it, or that it can't be done. Find people who will encourage you and support you along the way, as you're discovering and developing your gift.

PART TWO

Developing the Gift: The Work of Life is to Develop Your Gift

CHAPTER FOUR

WORK: THE MASTER KEY TO SUCCESS

"Hard work beats talent when talent
doesn't work hard."

—Kevin Durant

What made Michael Jordan, Walt Disney, and Colin Powell household names? Was it their intellect? Was it something they possessed that was specially given to them, something that others didn't have? Well, as each of their biographies reveal, they each felt there was nothing so special about themselves. Michael Jordan, one of the greatest basketball players the world has ever seen, was told he wasn't good enough to make his high school team. Walt Disney was fired from his first job because they thought he was "uncreative," and Colin Powell was a C- student.

What made these men household names? When it came to living their dreams, maximizing their potential, and fulfilling their God-given purpose, they had what I call "work stamina." Using the medium of the gift they were born with, coupled with an attitude of perseverance and dogged determination to live their dreams, they chose to succeed in their domains. They didn't just *want* to succeed; they *needed* to succeed as desperately as they needed oxygen. They were willing to sacrifice immediate gratification, and every day they made decisions to stick it out until they each reached their desired goals.

In our society today, we are increasingly placing more value on talent and educational intellect than on good, old-fashioned work ethic. We are moving away from a culture with core values of hard work and perseverance, to one that believes that being smart or talented grants you quick success. As proof of this, our media elevates those with the "it factor"—when the truth is, most of the truly successful people possess the "work factor." They have stamina, tenacity, and grit to account for the success they have. Remember that hard work will always beat talent when talent becomes lazy.

What separates high achievers from low achievers is not an extraordinary gift, but perseverance and work ethic. History continues to show us that the figures we most admire because of their inspirational stories of success were often able to overcome heartbreaking obstacles. These people may have only had modest natural giftings, but their work ethic and stamina—their ability to be disciplined, and their attitude of optimism—set them apart from their peers and made history.

The beauty about this is, no matter what our gift is, work stamina is within our reach.

Work Ethic

If you grew up in a challenging environment like I did, you know that you *had to work hard*, or else you wouldn't have food, clothing, or other necessities. This survival mentality can create a lot of stress (especially unnecessary stress in children) but it can also develop a great work ethic at a very young age.

My mom ran her own grocery business in our community in Ghana, and my brother and I walked from neighborhood to neighborhood selling groceries. It was hard work, and, to be honest, we didn't have a choice. Sometimes sales were very slow. Sometimes we were exhausted by the end of the day, since we carried all the different food items in the hot sun, walking miles just to make a sale. Also, unlike America, where running water is easily accessible, we had to walk miles just to fetch water and carry it on our heads. It was a tough job for kids! But it taught us *how* to work hard. And we were able to see the results of our hard work every time we made a sale. That consistent positive reinforcement instilled in us at a young age created a confidence in our abilities that would serve us well as we grew up and became independent.

My mother—the hardest-working woman I know—made the biggest impact on my understanding of a good work ethic. She did everything she could to put food on the table for us, even when it was difficult (which was most of the time), she did her best. When my dad became an alcoholic and stopped taking care of us, my mom took the responsibility upon her shoulders and raised her four children as a single mother. That meant going to the market, running her grocery business, and doing whatever she could to feed us—with no help except what we, as kids, were able to provide. So I was very much aware of her attitude and hard work growing up, and I believe that's where my work ethic comes from.

If you have a relative or a friend who modeled a great work ethic for you, thank them for setting such a great example for you to follow. They'll appreciate the fact that you took notice, and you can continue to learn from them. Even better, when you have developed a good work ethic, you'll be modeling it for others, whether you intend to or not. You never know who you might inspire along the way with your actions and words.

Now if you didn't have a good example of work ethic, how do you develop it? First you must ask yourself, "What is the purpose of developing a good work ethic?" You can't just work hard for the sake of it and expect to receive full benefits. Sure, hard work has its own rewards—it can develop consistency, mental stamina, confidence, and dependability. But there has to be a greater purpose and a *reason* for working hard, or else you may just work yourself into a rut with nothing much to show for it except calloused hands and a fatigued body. The secret is this: the best reason for having a good work ethic isn't self-serving; it is *others-serving*.

Find your personal motivation. Are you going to work hard so that you can provide for your family? Do you want to work hard to be able to donate money to a charity or to an individual in need? Do you want to become the best in your field so you can one day mentor others? Yes, you may gain financial benefits, accolades from your peers, awards for service, and a big ego boost—but is that really enough to satisfy your heart? For some, the answer is yes. For others, their lives would be incomplete if they weren't able to help and mentor individuals in their sphere of influence.

Remember, a good work ethic has many rewards; one of those is to be able to pour into the lives of those around you.

Work Versus a Job

Many times we confuse our divinely inspired *work* with our income-producing *job*. Is there really a difference? Absolutely! Work is what we are *given* to do—our task in life—and it doesn't always come with a paycheck. A job is what we *find* to do to provide income. This may seem like a very small difference, but the implications are vast.

Think about the terminology used in your workplace. We call our jobs our "work." We say, "I'm going to work now," or "I'll do that after work." And when we lose our jobs, we say, "I am out of work." But that's not true. If you lost your job recently or you are out of work right now, I want to assure you that you're not "out of work." You're merely out of a job for the moment. You cannot be fired from your work—your purpose. Though it may take longer than you'd like, you can always find another job, even if you have to create it yourself.

Don't believe me yet? Let's get down to the details.

The word *work* in Hebrew is *abad*. It's also the Greek word *ergon*. Both mean "to become, to bring to pass, to serve, to reveal, or to manifest." In other words, the word *work* means "to discover and become that which is already inside you"—*your gift* through self-manifestation. A gift without work will remain dormant potential. Work is the process used to manifest your gift and talents, and it helps you to discover achievements through your endurance.

See, we have been taught that *work* is something we *do*. Instead, we should be teaching that *work* is the process of becoming who you are meant to be. A job is merely a means of making money. Yes, both require a good work ethic, and I'm not saying that a job is something to be taken lightly. Unless we are independently wealthy, we all need them! But a job shouldn't *define* you, especially when so many people today are unhappy with their jobs.

Here are some fascinating (and discouraging) statistics regarding job satisfaction worldwide:[6]

- 87 percent of people in the world do not like their job;
- 50 percent do not feel satisfied or fulfilled;
- 25 percent say that their job is the number-one source of stress in their lives;

- 41 percent of people in the world are living from paycheck to paycheck;
- 70 percent are not motivated by what they do;
- 50 percent are underpaid;
- 67 percent are in the wrong field; and
  72 percent are in a place where they have been undermined so they will not succeed.

With such negative views of our jobs, it's no wonder we let our careers dictate our happiness! If we define ourselves by our jobs and we're unhappy with our current job situation, how can we lead low-stress, meaningful lives? *We can't.* Unless we change our understanding of what a job is and what work really means.

If you are motivated by the pursuit of money, greed will dominate and control your actions. But if you are motivated and empowered by the calling for your life, God's assignment will control you. We are not meant to be good job-keepers, but good workers.

The truth of the matter is that, in today's workplace, you can always be fired or replaced. You can lose your job. But you can't lose your life's work. You can't be fired from it, nor can someone replace you. Whatever talents, gifts, and strengths you were born with—that's what you were born with! It doesn't matter how many times you move around; you will still have what you were born with. It will not wear out, and it will not disappear. Nobody can take your life assignment away from you.

If you need a little more convincing, here are some valuable truths that will help you see how *work* differs from a *job*:

- Your job is what you were trained to do, but your work is what you were born to do.
- Your job is your career, but your work is your life assignment.
- Your job is your skill, but your work is your gift.

- You can be fired from your job, but you can never be fired from your work.
- Jobs are temporary. Work is permanent.
- You can retire from your job, but you cannot retire from your work, because your work is your *gift*.[7]

Your work is not your job.

You were not born just to make a living; you were born to make a difference in the world. The world needs you! Your neighbor needs you, and you need your neighbor. You may not know what your purpose is yet, but it is in there. God knows and He wants to show you. Your life purpose (work) may seem to be in seed form right now, but if you search your heart and pay attention to your gifts, your strengths, and your interests, you will discover your work—your gift.

Just remember: your work reveals your gift, and a job provides the paycheck.

Life Before—and After—Work

One of the greatest lessons I have learned came from one of the richest men who ever lived—King Solomon. He said, "Sow your seed in the morning, and at evening let not your hands be idle, for you do not know which will succeed, whether this or that, or whether both will do equally well."[8]

What does he mean? He means that we should spend our time being productive. In the morning, we should go to work and focus on our company's goals. Then in the evening, especially if we have a home business or personal vision, we should work on our own business instead of spending that valuable time watching

TV, surfing the Internet, or engaging in dead-end activities that waste our time.

The truth is, if you work for someone else, your future actually begins after five p.m. From 9 to 5, you don't really *own* your life. If you have a 9-to-5 job, you cannot grow and work on your future while you're at work, because that would be a mismanagement of your time and seen as dishonest.

When you get home from your job, that's your time to start thinking, dreaming, imagining, working, developing, refining, and enhancing your gift. The sooner you put this into practice, the sooner you will reap the rewards!

I began working this plan when I signed my professional soccer deal, and I still do it today with great results. I work for a fitness club called Emerald City Athletics. I'm constantly inspiring, empowering, and equipping people by building a vision for them and helping them reach their fitness goals. I love what I do!

From 9 a.m. to 6 p.m., all my energy and focus is given to Emerald City Athletics. But the waking hours before and after work are all mine. I wake up 5 a.m. and I work on my own business until 8:45 a.m. On average, I work between two to three hours each day on my own business. It may not seem like much, but it adds up to sometimes fifteen hours a week! That's a part-time job…all done before 9 a.m.

When I get home from work, spending quality time with my wife is my number-one priority. I want to be the best husband, and someday the best father to our children, and I choose to spend my evenings at home relaxing instead of working.

My life begins long before 9 a.m. What about you?

No matter the schedule your normal day takes, please heed the advice given by Solomon and don't let your hands be idle. Don't allow unimportant time-suckers to destroy your life and keep you from your destiny.

What True Wealth Really Means

As you know by now, abundance doesn't only mean financial abundance. You can have abundance in wealth, but if you have all kinds of health problems, are you really wealthy? If your family and children are all struggling while you have lots of money, are you really wealthy? Abundance here goes beyond money and material things—it encompasses health, family, business, and spiritual life.

As we see in our own circle of family, friends, and coworkers, many people shape their lives around their jobs. So their jobs dictate when they take vacation, what time they eat, how many hours they put in each day, and how many years they need to put in before they retire—and quit working! These people are frustrated because their jobs have taken away their energy, strength, stamina, and passion from them. Even worse, they know within themselves that they were created to do something very important—they were just never able to do that specific thing because they felt they had to put in every waking moment at their job.

And since we start indoctrinating our children early on—telling them how they'll need to get an education and get a job—we should take the time to explain to them the differences between work and a job, as well as taking the time to encourage their gifts. Every child is filled with untapped potential, talents, and gifts waiting to be deployed, and we need to encourage this more than ever so that, when they are

All great achievers are given multiple reasons to believe they are failures. But in spite of that they persevere. In the face of adversity, rejection, and failings, they continue believing in themselves and refuse to consider themselves failures.

—John C. Maxwell

ready to enter the workforce, they know not to let a job define them and control their entire life.

Here's the reality: We were never meant to spend our days punching the clock to be accountable to somebody else. We're meant to work, but we are often too tired from our jobs to do *our work*. After a long career in our jobs, we retire with great aspirations but find that we are either too tired, too old, or too unmotivated to do the *work* we always wanted to do. Far too often, the dream dies unrealized because a lifetime was spent on the job, and not at work.

I know I don't want to die with my gifts unopened, my dreams never realized. I imagine you don't want to die with your dreams still inside you either. We must understand our true wealth—our gifts, our families, our passions—and spend the rest of our days in pursuit of it—the best kind of abundance.

CHAPTER FIVE

LIVING A LIFE OF PURPOSE

> "The greatest tragedy in life is not death but a life
> without a purpose."
> —Myles Munroe

Caution! This chapter may stretch your thinking and provoke you in a positive, transforming, and empowering way. It may also require that you evaluate some of your deeply held beliefs, and that you take stock of where you are and *where you want to be.*

We've learned that every manmade product is designed to fulfill a specific function—a purpose. We've also learned that every human being was born for a purpose, which is defined as original intent. God created *everything* to fulfill a specific purpose. This means that nothing exists just for the fun of it or by random chance—even mosquitoes. We might not understand a mosquito's purpose (other than to pester us and make us itch), but it has one, because *nothing* is designed without a purpose. Now, if God created the mosquito for a purpose, how much more is there a purpose for humans—God's apex of creation?

You are not an accident, a mistake, or an experiment. You are not a sophisticated primate dancing to your DNA, and you are certainly not the result of time plus matter plus chance.

Now that we see we have been given a great gift and a great responsibility, how do we live up to our potential?

Questions from the Heart

When I was a kid, back in Ghana, I became obsessed with the desire to know the meaning of life. I wanted to know what *invisible something* separated truly successful people from everyone else. In my world, there were those who had (the minority) and those who didn't have (the majority). Since I was a have-not, I wanted to understand why there was so much poverty around us and why only a few people seemed to be successful. Even as a little boy, I had big questions: Does my existence have any purpose, or am I here just by chance? Why was I placed on this planet? *What is my purpose?*

I wanted answers. I also wanted a better life for me, my family, and my country.

Our culture today presents a variety of answers from the media, movies, advertisements, education, science, and even religion about what it means to be human. Some people will tell you that human beings are nothing more than biology.

One of the so-called leading atheists today is Richard Dawkins at Oxford University. Regarding his belief of what humans beings really are, he writes, "Life is matter and only matter. We are survival machines, robot vehicles, blindly programmed to preserve the selfish molecules of DNA known as genes. The only purpose of life is DNA survival. A person is nothing more than DNA's way of making more DNA like itself."[9] What a depressing thought! If we are nothing more than selfish robots with the desire to procreate, how has the world not ended already? What in the world would we really have to live for?

Francis Crick, another atheist who discovered DNA with his coworker back in the 1950s, wrote these words: "Your joy and your sorrows, your memory and your ambition, your sense of personal identity and free will, are in fact no more than the behavior of a vast assembly of nerve cells and their associated molecules." This sounds so deeply impersonal, void of any purpose. Imagine if we just went through life with no direction, no real goals—what would be the reason for getting out of bed each day? Yet that's what it feels like to live without purpose—or rather, to live while *ignoring* your purpose.

The Tragedy of Life without Purpose

One day, my best friend and I were discussing whether there was something more tragic than death. According to my friend, nothing is more tragic than losing our loved ones. So is there anything more tragic in life than death? Indeed, I believe it is more tragic to be alive and not know why, than to be dead.

If you don't know why you are living and you are not in pursuit of this answer, then your time is being wasted. Our world is filled with so many people who are alive, but don't know why they are living, and that's why waking up every morning is so hard. They hate Monday morning, and they would love to stay in bed and sleep forever because, when you are asleep, you don't have to think about life—the struggles, the pain. But these people can't fully celebrate the amazing parts of life either, if they don't have any concept of purpose.

Mankind is often a walking contradiction. We are long on duration but short on donation. We want to live long, but we don't want to grow old. We don't want to embrace old age with grace; we want plastic surgery to fool other people into thinking we're younger. Because let's face it—*we're not fooling ourselves.*

We get the big house we've dreamt of for thirty years, and then the house depresses us—it's too much space to clean, or too expensive to keep up. We finally get that expensive car we worked night and day to buy, and then we hate it when we see someone with a newer model. We dream of marriage, and then we get into it, encounter disagreements, and can't wait to get divorced. We aspire to get more degrees than a thermometer, and then when we get them and they didn't land us in our dream jobs, we're in debt and miserable. Wealth becomes a burden without a purpose, and poverty becomes a source of frustration without a purpose. We are running after material things at the expense of meaning. But without *meaning*, it all means nothing.

I believe we're meant for greater things. So how do we stop this vicious cycle of wanting, needing, and achieving, only to remain unfulfilled? The change starts at home.

Tired Teachings of Tradition

From an early age, we are taught the traditional way—go to school, get a degree, get a job. But we are not taught to discover our purpose. Without purpose, education simply becomes a wall of detention, instead of a hallway to great intentions.

Everywhere we look, the youth are confused, the old are frustrated, the rich are bored, the poor are depressed, the teenagers are angry, the intellectuals are disillusioned, the scientists are perplexed, the religious are redundant, and the Christians are burned out. Everybody is sick and tired—because they have no sense of destiny.

Even if you are a Christian, it doesn't mean that you have found your purpose. Some of the most frustrated people in the world are church-going, Bible-reading people. In fact, I bet one or two people just popped into your mind while reading that! These people love church, but they use church as a cover-up; it gives them a break from reflecting with introspection of why they are living. They may love the preoccupation of worship and preaching because they are afraid that when it stops, they have to go out into the real world and figure out why they are living. Salvation doesn't mean you automatically know your purpose. You still have to work to find it, nurture it, and share it. And if you find yourself in an environment that stunts your growth, you must do the work of removing yourself from it and finding the right environment.

Our society is filled with people who love *the idea* of becoming something. We love the idea of becoming a professional athlete, but not the responsibility and fitness demands that come with it. We love the idea of becoming rich, but we don't want to work hard. So where does that leave us? Sadly, many people will never move past *the idea* of becoming anything at all.

Investing twenty, thirty, or even seventy years into *nothingness* is an absolute tragedy. Even five years of your life is too long to be doing something you were not created to do—or to be avoiding *what you were* created to do. Though it can be hard, you can't allow yourself to be manipulated and massaged by your culture, family, or the education system into a position that is not in line with your purpose. These people may want the best for you, but they are not in charge of your purpose or your destiny—only you are. And you must take responsibility for it.

If you're struggling with your purpose right now, this may sound like a life-or-death decision. And, in some ways, it is. You have the power to speak life or death into your dreams and purpose. But instead of being scared of change, uncertain of the future, and hesitant to speak up for yourself, maybe a simple change in your mind-set is all that is needed.

Instead of needing to be reactive to your circumstances, be proactive instead. You make the next move; don't let it be made for you. Instead of viewing your future as a great and scary unknown, see it as an exciting adventure—because it absolutely is! The sooner you step up and step into your purpose, the more doors will open, and the more answers you will find.

Five Questions That Control the Human Race

Now that we're getting excited to take charge of our own journeys and discover our purposes, we can gain a head start if we understand the five questions that control the entire human race. I first read these questions in a book by Dr. Myles Munroe, a man who has had a great influence on my life. I discovered these truths when I was twenty-two years old, and I can guarantee you that they will still be valid when I am ninety-two.

As you read these questions and my explanations, know that you are one among seven billion people on planet earth today who is on a search. We are all searching, whether we know it or not; the answers to these questions are what bring true fulfillment in every area of our lives. They dominate everything we do, including our environment, economy, family, and even the destruction of our family. Simply, they are the questions of the human heart:

1. *Who am I?*
More often than not, when I ask people, "Who are you?" they tell me what they *do for a living*. But I didn't ask them what they do. I want to know who they *are*. This is a question of identity, and even though it should be easy—*I am a parent. A wife. A husband. A son. An aunt. An animal lover. A Christian*—we are taught to answer this question by naming our job, as if that is truly what defines us. And we now know that's *not at all* what should define us.

So how do you identify yourself? What roles and responsibilities do you fulfill in your daily life? What are you passionate about? *Who* are you?

2. *Where am I from?*

Humanity has been trying to answer this question for over three thousand years. Some say that humans came from monkeys (which came from primordial slime that became a salamander that became a tadpole that developed into a frog, which eventually became an ape that became a human), trying to explain it through evolution. Some say humans came from a big bang that caused some genetic coding in the abyss of six million years ago. Regardless of how you believe humans got here, where you are from is not a question of your ethnic and cultural background. It is a question of your origin, your beliefs, and your primary influences.

3. *Why am I here?*

This is a question that still eludes many people because they believe the question of purpose can be exhausted. Why are you here? Why were you conceived? Is there a reason for your life? It's a tragedy that, by some estimates, nearly 90 percent of the world's seven billion people haven't answered this question.

If we look at the basics, when sexual intercourse takes place, and the sperm of a man enters into the woman, over six hundred million sperm rush toward the egg—and only one makes it. That one is *you*. Was there a purpose for the divine Creator to chose that one sperm, for you to come at this time? Is there something great for which you are here to accomplish?

Sadly, our education system, our culture, and our family tells us that we came here to simply make a living, pay bills, maybe have a family, and die. That's false. You came here to make an impact and deposit something that the world is supposed to enjoy—and you have to discover what that thing is.

4. *What can I do?*

Did you know that a very large percent of the population on earth is living far below their true potential and will die without fully realizing their true ability? We don't know what we are capable of doing because we don't know our Source, and we have accepted other people's opinions, philosophies, and concepts of our true ability. We have allowed our history, culture, and education to tell us what we can and cannot do. But what is your *true capacity*?

If you allow it, other people will put a limit on your true potential. And sometimes, because of fear or uncertainty, you may try to put a limit on your own potential. But don't do it! Push the limits; see how far you really can go. I'm willing to bet you'll surprise yourself if you keep moving forward.

5. *Where am I going?*

This is a question of destiny. Where is your future address in life? Where will you be in the next five or fifteen years? What do you see for the next sixty years of your life? Who do you dream of becoming? What's your vision?

You are not here to just throw a single pebble into the ocean of humanity and go unnoticed. You are here to deposit something that required your birth—and that is not done yet. You were born to live with purpose, and until you find your personal reason for waking up every morning, you will never be fulfilled.

The misunderstanding of true identity is why a man will work two jobs, abandoning his children and frustrating his wife. He tries to find his identity by competing with other people to buy nice cars and nice clothes so that *he feels accepted.*

But you don't need any of these things to be accepted or to know where you're going. You only need some determination and a plan or a dream.

Now What?

Purpose is the key to life. It's the key to business, to fulfillment, to meaning, to significance, to leadership, to greatness, and to learning how to be productive. It is the key to serving your gift. *You already have it*; you just have to tap into it.

Three thousand years ago, a man named Solomon had more wisdom than anybody on the earth during his time. He was sought after, and audiences came from distant lands just to hear his advice. When he was chosen to be a king of a people, God appeared to him and told him to ask for anything he wanted and it would be done. Unlike our likely answers today, Solomon never asked for money, a house, clothes, or any of the material things we seek after. He asked for knowledge, understanding, and wisdom, and they were given to him.

During his reign, he wrote a book called Proverbs, in which he made a statement that changed my life. He said, "Many are the plans in a man's heart, but the Lord's purpose for that man will prevail." What does Solomon mean? He means that we too often go through life talking about our own plans—the work we want to do, the place we want to live, the school we want to go to. We have ideas for all the things we want to do—but, in the end, the Creator has His purpose for us, and His purpose will prevail over everything we plan.

I learned three important principles from Solomon's statement:

1. Purpose is more important than plans.
2. Purpose precedes plans.
3. Purpose is more powerful than our plans.
4. Purpose will prevail over plans.

Until you discover His purpose for your life, your own plans will not make much sense, and you will not have great success.

Your plans should be made in accordance to His purpose for your life. And they will always require you to share your gift with others.

CHAPTER SIX

SHARING YOUR GIFT

"The value of our gift is maximized when we share it
with others."

—Michael Tetteh

Soccer is a team sport. On the field, each team is required
to have eleven players: ten field players and one goalkeeper.
While some players can play multiple positions, each individual
selected for the team is gifted at one position in which he excels.
When each player is playing the appropriate position, at the
right time, blending within the formation and sharing the ball, a
beautiful game emerges.

If each individual is encouraged to express his unique gift at
the right time on the field that is what makes the beautiful game
of soccer so exciting to watch. The same can be said about life.

When a player tries to do everything and doesn't want to
share the ball, a certain selfishness is revealed that robs other
players from expressing their true gifts. These games are difficult
to watch, as it seems like the entire stadium can see what the
player in question cannot. The same happens in life when others

over-prove or allow their egos to overstep the boundaries of their God-given gift.

The game of soccer reveals an important principle about the way our gifts are meant to be used. The blending, support, diversity, interdependence, and unity displayed in the game of soccer reveal how life is intended to function. In the game of soccer, when the ball is shared between the players, we see not only the strength, but also the maximization of gifts, skills, and potential of each player. The sharing of our gifts is the Creator's way of revealing His purposes and plans for humanity.

Sharing Fulfills a Higher Purpose

The Rainbow Fish, a children's book by Marcus Pfister, tells the story of the most beautiful fish in the ocean. His scales were every shade of blue, green, and purple, with sparkling silver scales mixed in. He was very beautiful, but he was also very selfish. He was so beautiful that he thought he was too good to play with the other fish in the ocean.

One day a little blue fish asked Rainbow Fish for one of his beautiful, shimmering scales—but he refused. Because of his selfishness, he was very unpopular with the other fish. He was not only the most beautiful fish in the ocean, but he was also the loneliest fish in the ocean.

He told Starfish about his problem, and Starfish sent him to talk to a wise old octopus. The octopus told Rainbow Fish that if he wanted to be happy, he should give one of his beautiful scales to each of the other fish. Rainbow Fish just could not imagine giving away his beautiful scales.

Once again, the little blue fish asked for one of Rainbow Fish's scales. He hesitated for a moment, but finally pulled off one of his scales and gave it to the little blue fish. When the other fish saw the little blue fish with a shiny scale, Rainbow Fish was surrounded by all the other fish asking for one of his shiny scales. Before he knew it, he had given away all of his shiny scales except for one. Suddenly, he realized that although he was no longer the most beautiful fish in the ocean, he was happier than ever before.

Be an Outlet, Not an Inlet

I love the story of the Rainbow Fish because it's a reminder that we were created to be an outlet and never an inlet. We are to share our time, talents, and treasures with others—not hoard them for ourselves.

In the biblical text, there are two important bodies of water: the Jordan River and the Dead Sea. Here's something I learned from these two bodies of water: The Jordan River flows into, and then through, the Sea of Galilee. It continues south, and flows into the Dead Sea. It starts as the same water from the same source—and yet one lake teems with life, and the other is dead.

The Dead Sea is so far below sea level that it has no outlet streams. The water flows in, but it does not flow out. Tons of water evaporate from the Dead Sea, but the minerals remain, causing the salt content to be so super-concentrated that only the most robust and miniscule organisms can live in the water.

The Sea of Galilee takes water from the Jordan River, and then it gives water. The water simply passes through the Sea of Galilee. As a result, the Sea of Galilee teems with life—all types of fish and plants grow there—and beauty.

The difference between the Dead Sea and the Sea of Galilee is that the Dead Sea is not an outlet. It doesn't feed into anything. It doesn't give water to anything. It only receives water, so it becomes stagnant. These two bodies of water reveal an important truth of human life. It is in receiving and then giving back that life and hope are sustained. Jesus, who journeyed around these two bodies of water, surely knew that giving was the key to life. That's why He freely gave and shared His life with us.

Our culture today is filled with too many people who just want to take and not give. As a result, they are dead inside. They are not giving anything, and their lives are salty. They are the walking dead.

Yet one act of giving makes you come alive. You have to walk through life relentlessly discovering what you're supposed to deposit to your world. What service are you supposed to bring? What fruit is the world waiting to eat from you?

> **Sharing is the greatest evidence of true freedom. It is more fruitful to give than to receive.**

Henry D. Strunk said, "Service is the rent we pay for the space we take up on earth." If you rent a house and don't pay your rent, you know what the landlord will do—kick you out! So why should we expect anything different from the ultimate Landlord? You are born to pay rent with your gift, your dreams, and your talents, which were placed inside of you before the foundation of the world. The more you give, the more you realize you can give. The more you give, the more you share, the more you love, the more compassion you show to mankind— the more your life has meaning. When you begin to view your life as a conduit for life—and not a reservoir for your gift to lie stagnant—that's when exceedingly great things begin to happen.

Each of Us Has a Responsibility to the Next Generation

In the book *The Element*, the author tells a story of a young girl who was prescribed medication because she couldn't concentrate in school. Her poor academic performance and inability to concentrate at school resulted in her teachers thinking she was impossible to manage. They were concerned that she might be suffering from a mental disorder.

It was suggested that she be placed on medication to calm her down. Sadly, there are too many stories of children who have been mistakenly placed on medication because parents and teachers haven't done the work necessary to help their children discern their true gifts. Thankfully, a psychiatrist saw that the little girl was not sick but born to dance. Her extreme spatial aptitude and acumen while moving simply did not translate well in the classroom. While certainly a challenge to overcome, it was not a challenge that required medication. All that was required was a refocusing on learning styles that did work, as opposed to the quick fix that prescribed drugs seem to promise. That little girl, Gillian Lynne, became one of the most accomplished dancers and choreographers in the world. And all because one man saw her potential and encouraged her mother to direct her daughter's energy into her daughter's gift.

One of the world's richest men was also nearly medicated as a child because he was evaluated as uneducable. As a little boy, Bill Gates was gifted in computer technology. Even at a very young age, he had a natural talent for science and math. All he wanted to do was create things and work on computers, but his creativity was nearly destroyed by his teachers.

He began to show signs of preteen rebelliousness that put him at odds with his mother. Then, when Bill was twelve, he began to be independent emotionally—some would call this a stubborn streak. This was very tough for his parents.

According to his biographer, young Bill was lost. He graduated from high school and was accepted to Harvard. In the fall of 1973, Bill said good-bye to his parents and moved from Seattle to Massachusetts to begin again as a freshman at Harvard— ready to major in law. Yet no subject or course study ignited his passion, imagination, creativity, and gift with computers. Well before college, his destiny has already been set.

He struggled with academics. While sometimes falling asleep during tests, he had no problem spending twenty-four hours at the Harvard computer center. He began to prioritize playing video games and poker over schoolwork. As a result, he dropped out of college just before his senior year. His parents were disappointed, but, fortunately for Bill, he had already seen and accepted his destiny. He saw his gift, believed in his gift, and went for it. Today, the entire world benefits from the efforts Bill Gates made to create Microsoft.

> **Our world's most inspiring leaders have risen above their circumstances in order to maximize their true gifts and dreams.**

What if Bill Gates had stayed in Harvard and become a lawyer? What if Gillian, the gifted dancer, took the suggested medication and stayed in school instead of traveling the world to share her gift with enthralled audiences? The world would be very different today—and these are just two people's stories! Imagine how you might change the world if you only harnessed your gift.

As you think about the endless possibilities, ask yourself these questions:

- In what ways have you initiated your talents?
- Can you describe some things—software, art, science, ideas, structures, medicine—you hope the next generation will be able to utilize when it comes to your particular gift?
- What risks have you taken for the sake of sharing your gift?

We should never settle for the norm because there are too many people who depend on our commitment to this principle. Just as Bill Gates and so many others have had a rebellious spirit, we too must declare independence from those who seek to limit, ignore, or diminish our true gifts and potential.

History is evidence that past generations have left us with many great inventions, artwork, technology, music, books, and achievements that we are still enjoying today and that are still making our lives a little easier. The gifts that were deposited in them have become a blessing of great benefit to us. Likewise, your gift, your natural talents, and your potential must be maximized so the next generation can benefit from it.

By maximizing our gifts to the fullest potential, we will be providing the next generation with a roadmap they can use to effectively realize their gifts. Without this roadmap, our children are forced to become consumers of *other people's gifts*. Once those resources are exhausted, people will have nothing left from which to grow and prosper. It starts with us.

Don't Be a Thief of Your Own Generation

One of the saddest things facing my country of Ghana (and the rest of the world) is the fact that our elders and leaders have not been leaving anything for the next generation. Unlike the leaders before them, they have become like the Dead Sea and are taking all they can from available resources, without any care or concern for what future generations will encounter in their wake.

Too many leaders insist on living lavishly and draining the pool of available resources. As a result, a country that should be prosperous barely survives, decade after decade. But I have found that those people who have shared and distributed their gifts as God instructed are less fearful of dying, and are certainly happier.

Everything in God's creation functions on the principle of receiving and releasing. Creation affects us, and we affect creation. Even more important, we were created to be interdependent on each other. God is a God of unity, but He is also the God of diversity. There is diversity within creation and within humans, and all this diversity has unity through interdependence. Therefore, every decision we make—to either share or not share our gifts—is personal, but certainly never *private*. Releasing and maximizing our gifts for the next generation is not an option. It is a necessary condition for our existence.

The sharing of talent becomes a logical behavior for those who have placed their ego aside for the greater good. As you contemplate your role in sharing your gifts, consider these questions:

- What gifts can you commit to sharing with others?
- How do you plan on sharing those gifts?

Be specific and start creating a plan so you can hold yourself accountable.

Live Full and Die Empty

God has been so faithful to me—even when I wasn't always faithful to Him. He's given me gifts and a vision that is bigger than myself—so big that I must share it with others.

While soccer will always be such a huge and meaningful part of my life, a nagging feeling encouraged me to think bigger than the sport that had defined me for so many years. I started asking myself if playing soccer would really help future generations. Not satisfied with my own hesitance, I applied more pressure and found some surprising answers that would lead me to a purpose I never could have imagined achieving. *My purpose is bigger than soccer.* My purpose is to deliver hope to others, through whatever means I have available. In that regard, soccer, although still a gift, was merely a vessel in my case.

As I thought about this, I pictured a very young me on a dirt field with my friends, clearing brush and strategizing all of the various ways that we could bring a thing called *hope* to our little village. Hope had come in the form of soccer. Now, with this new realization regarding my true gift and talent, I was more equipped than ever to utilize it through all of my experiences.

Over the years, life has humbled me and allowed me to see the responsibility I have to contribute something back to the world. The day I committed to sharing my gift with the world was the day I found myself. From that moment onward, every past struggle and every bump in the road became signs that were impossible to ignore.

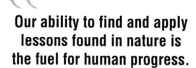

Our ability to find and apply lessons found in nature is the fuel for human progress.

These days, I'm working to establish a school back in Ghana, and I spend a good bit of time traveling to high schools and colleges to speak to young people about potential. God took me from my home; I had to leave my family and friends to get knowledge and understanding and wisdom and use my gift. I had to be in the right environment for my exact gift!

Every single human being is a treasure chest. You came to earth loaded. However, if you don't maximize your time, you're going to get closer to the cemetery. If you wait too long, you will not be able to deposit your treasure to your generation or the next.

The idea of the cemetery being the richest place on earth truly changed my life. On the day I heard that story, I made an agreement with the cemetery: I'm not taking anything to the cemetery until I have released everything deposited in me to the world. I encourage you to make this agreement too.

Maybe you have been gifted with writing, or you're gifted as an athlete, a dancer, a computer genius, or an amazing singer.

Maybe you have been ignoring, postponing, or neglecting the awesome treasure of potential deposited in you. Whether you are five years old or ninety-five, it doesn't matter: The fact that you are still breathing is proof that you are still carrying something unique, powerful, and amazing that the world needs, and that future generations are going to benefit from. It is imperative that you maximize your fullest gift and potential for the sake of the next generation.

Live full, actively making a difference in the lives of others.

Die empty, knowing you did your best with your gift and your time on earth.

CHAPTER SEVEN

WHO IS THE GREATEST?

*"If any man seeks for greatness, let him forget
greatness and ask for truth, and he will find both."*
—Horace Mann

You were born to be great. You are intended to dominate and to lead in your area of expertise. You also possess the potential to manifest your greatness.

If your reaction to these statements is, "Not me," you are not alone. Most people do not believe that they have greatness trapped within them, or that they have the potential to do more than their current circumstances would indicate. Our society devalues us in one way or the other, and worst of all is the mental conditioning that affects us even in the best circumstances.

I have met many people on my journey who believe they cannot become great, but I always tell them, "You can, you should, and you must because your generation is in need of your gift!" Know that true greatness starts with accepting your significance and knowing that your significance is a product of your value. Your value lies in your gift that must be used in service to the world.

Don't Misunderstand the Meaning

Too many misunderstand the meaning of *greatness*. Because we feel true greatness is reserved for people "better than" us, or at least more well-known than we are, we run the risk of never really discovering our true potential. Most cultures perceive greatness through the lens of materialism: status, position, economic success, educational degrees, fame, and popularity. So in order to rediscover our *traditional concepts* of greatness, we need to look at people like Bill Gates, Steve Jobs, Martin Luther King, Jr., Michael Jordan, Abraham Lincoln, Mahatma Gandhi, Henry Ford, Mother Teresa, Nelson Mandela, Walt Disney, Helen Keller, and Pablo Picasso—not for their fame...but for what they accomplished.

In my studies of these influential leaders, I discovered that their greatness was never a result of their education, socioeconomic status, or superior upbringing—their greatness had nothing to do with their educational degrees, status, titles, or fame. None of them made it a goal to be great or sought after greatness as their mission. They all went searching for the truth about themselves and preoccupied themselves with their gift, while in service to their generation. This means true greatness or leadership has more to do with self-discovery. Their greatness was a *product* of discovering a gift, refining that gift, developing that gift, immersing themselves in that gift, and deploying their unique gift to the world around them.

Greatness is good and necessary for the human spirit. It's inherently built in us to crave it so passionately that it moves us to develop and create the "uncreatable." This desire is the very source of our purpose and inspiration to live meaningful and fulfilled lives. It's what ignites development and advancement, and is the birthplace for inventions.

How to Become Great

My parents will tell you that, from an early age, I wanted to be great. I was blessed to find my gift early on as a child, and I didn't want to do anything else. Yet, over the years, I ran into a big stumbling block—other people! You may have encountered the very same obstacle.

Even my parents advised me not to crave the sport that I felt defined me. My friends told me I would never become great. And then, worst of all, I had my coach, a respected professional, whom I idolized for over five years, tell me that, in his opinion, I wasn't good enough to be a professional soccer player. The poverty mentality and the environment that surrounded me encouraged me to feel that greatness was only for the chosen few in society—and I was not one of the chosen few in their eyes. Still I refused to believe that greatness was reserved for a segment of society far beyond my reach.

As long as you are a human, greatness is knocking at your door. That means the young boy and girl living in a tiny mud hut in the villages of Africa, that man or woman sleeping under the tree or bridge in Seattle, and those people sleeping in the twenty-million-dollar ocean-view homes in Montecito all have seeds of greatness inside them.

Giftocracy is all about serving the world through your gift. In the cultures of this world, we often control, manipulate, exploit, and capitalize on other people in order to lead and to be great. But that's not how it works—at least, it shouldn't be. If you want to be great—if you want to be first—then there is one thing you must do: you must serve others.

- The truly great are willing to serve.
- The truly great take initiative and don't run from responsibility.

- The truly great are called on often because of prior service.
- The truly great are never bored or lazy.
- The truly great do not complain about their greatness.
- The truly great do not seek to be truly great.
- The truly great are really missed when they are gone.
- The truly great are willing to make sacrifices that most would not make.

Greatness Is Measured by Service

The philosophy of *Giftocracy* is based on the leadership philosophy introduced two thousand years ago. Jesus radically shifts our priorities and concepts by saying, "The one who is the greatest among you must become like the youngest, and the leader like the servant." Most of the time, we have this backwards!

One of the best examples of *Giftocracy* and servant-leadership I've come across is the interaction between Jesus and His students. He told His students to prepare a place so He could eat the Passover meal with them, so they prepared a place to eat with their Master. What was significant about this was that, in their culture and in those days, it was required that, before people shared a meal at the table, a guest's feet must be washed by the host.

On this particular occasion, nobody had stepped up to wash the feet of the disciples when they came into the house. Their mode of transportation was walking, and they would have walked for miles in their sandals. By the time they had arrived at the host's house, they would have carried in all of the dust, mud, and sand from their journey. And now they were about to eat with dirty feet!

Jesus noticed that their feet were dirty and that no one had taken the responsibility to wash their feet. Perhaps they were so hungry or tired (or both) that they weren't thinking, but none of them had even *thought about* serving the others.

What did Jesus do? He laid down His garment, took a towel, dipped it into a bowl of water, and began to wash their feet. Even after this beautiful act of service, His students began to argue again, after supper, about who was considered the greatest—even after Jesus told them about His impending death. How selfish!

The attitude of the students reminds me of modern-day funerals and how death can tear families apart. When a family member is about to die—often weeks or months before they've even passed away—people start thinking of what they will get, and the ugly fights to get Mom's watch or Dad's company take priority over paying true homage to the person they have loved and revered for years.

Sadly, this attitude is pervasive in our society today. Everybody wants to know what he is going to get, what he can take, what's coming in his direction, how he will be established, and who is next in line. Everybody wants to be next to get *something*. This happens in our families, in our marriages, and in our businesses.

Instead of demanding others to serve us, or expecting to get something from someone, let's put our garments aside, humble ourselves, and serve our gift to the world.

Six Principles of Greatness

The words *servant* and *greatness*, when put together, seem like opposites, yet that's the principle Jesus is teaching us. I have studied and meditated on this connection, and have deduced the meaning of *greatness* into six principles:

1. *Greatness is preordained; it is not a preference.*
You were born to be great and to manifest your greatness. Greatness, therefore, is not something you do but who you are.

Just as a bird cannot retire from flight, so you cannot retire from yourself.

There is a prepared place for each human on this planet. Your unique, gifted domain cannot be taken from you, and you cannot take it from somebody else.

2. *Greatness is a prepared position.*

There's a domain set aside for all. You don't have to go anywhere looking for it because God predestined your domain long before He made you. This understanding will free people from jealousy, competition, envy, a scarcity mind-set, and every negative emotion you can think of.

You cannot compete with a person whom God has prepared a place for. Instead of wasting your time competing with others for positions of prestige, power, and leadership, spend your time seeking God to reveal your already-prepared place.

3. *Greatness is innate.*

Many times, we ask God for things He has already given us. But you cannot send a prayer request to God to give you greatness. You came to earth with your greatness trapped inside you. Whether you embrace, develop, and serve your gift is totally your choice.

4. *Greatness is a heavenly deposit.*

Jesus taught His students that they couldn't request somebody's domain or position—they couldn't appeal for any position of power and prestige because it's not His to give. Many times, we think some preacher, CEO, parent, or teacher can *make us great*. Don't waste your time on that. The position you are seeking cannot be given to you by anybody. God has already arranged your spot for you.

5. *Greatness demands a price.*

Your greatness was established before the foundation of the world. However, fulfilling it comes with a price not everybody is willing to pay. Many times, we see and read stories about people who became great (in reality, they simply discovered their gift and developed their greatness) and many of us are envious of them; but we don't really know their stories very well. We hear about famous people and wealthy people, and we want to have what they have. But we never pause to ask what it took for them to be where they are and to become who they are.

I'm always interested to learn from stories of great men and women who paid the price to be where they are. Indeed, you are born to be great, but until you are willing to pay the price to be great, your greatness will never be manifested.

6. *Greatness is to be shared with others; it is not just for you to keep.*

You were born to serve others with your gift, and the discovery of your gift births your greatness. The word *greatness* describes a person who has achieved great things. They are great on the inside—they have a way about them that empowers, inspires, enlarges, and adds value to others. More importantly, they have a heart to serve others.

When I'm around a person of greatness, I'm very humbled by their gift, yet I'm also inspired. Even though they realize that they might have accomplished something wonderful in their lives, they are more focused on unlocking the greatness that's trapped inside others. Greatness has more to do with self-discovery and self-manifestation for others.

We should always celebrate the greatness in others and encourage them to do even greater things. And we should celebrate the greatness in ourselves—constantly working, refining, and enduring—to ensure that our character matches our gift.

The price for greatness demands suffering. Suffering is a product of endurance. Endurance is a product of character. And character produces hope.

CHAPTER EIGHT

LEADING FROM YOUR GIFT

"An army of sheep, led by a lion, can defeat an army
of lions, led by a sheep."
—Ghanaian Proverb

I f we truly want to understand how to become effective leaders
and serve our organizations, companies, churches, families,
and nations well, where should we look to learn leadership? Many
search for CEOs with fancy titles—perhaps they can learn from
their experiences. Some look to the world of political leaders.
Still others examine it from the world of business and consultants
to learn leadership. To go one step further, the majority goes to
school to learn the *principles* behind leadership, or at least the
often-outdated theories. But where can we get real-life, hands-on
training?

The Desperate Need for Leadership

Nothing is more urgently needed right now than effective
leadership. Most, if not all, of our nations are challenged

economically, socially, culturally, and financially. Of all the obstacles we are facing (such as corruption, wars, terrorism, and corporate greed), the greatest need we are faced with is to find true and effective leaders to confront these issues.

Africa is looking for effective leadership. The United States is looking for effective leadership. Europe is looking for effective leadership. Interestingly, it's not like we don't have people with leadership titles and positions occupying offices. The truth is, we have too many leaders but very few who understand leadership.

There are seven major domains of influence in our society: religion, economics, government, family, education, media, and sports. These areas all claim to have leaders, yet I'm left to wonder what kind of world we are building now for generations to come.

Internationally renowned communicator and author John C. Maxwell said, "Everything rises and falls on leadership." What does that mean? It means nothing develops, progresses, advances, or succeeds without leadership involvement. Nothing changes without leadership. In other words, leadership is the key that determines everything that happens. Companies, countries, families, nations, churches, and organizations are only as good their leader—and as effective as their leadership. And as you can tell by the state of things all over the world right now, true leadership is a lost art.

It's Greek to Me—Out with Old Ideas

Our leaders keep failing because they have been taught by dead men's ideas. After all the courses they took in management, psychology, and leadership, they keep seeing failure after failure. In our desire to be leaders, we control people, own people, manipulate people, and believe we own those we lead. This is not leadership. This is actually sophisticated dictatorship.

The Greek thinkers have truly brainwashed our schools. Our schools are filled with books by Plato, Aristotle, and Socrates, and their ideas have been engrained in our heads to make us perfect followers. In fact, IQ tests have been introduced to further separate followers from leaders. Brilliant opposing ideas—especially those capable of resuscitating the developing world—have been dismissed and nullified. They have been described as the shallow rants of the disgruntled or semiliterate.

Just think of how many times you have you been told that you are incapable of learning, incapable of succeeding, or incapable of being a true leader. But those are lies! Your leadership is internal! It's not outside of you. It's trapped in your seed, your gift. That means your leadership potential is inherent because you were created with it—by the Creator Himself.

Many people speak negatively about the Bible. I can't speak to your experiences, but reading the Bible changed my life. I discovered that I was born to be a leader, that my life had meaning, and that I possess the capacity to manifest my greatness. I learned through the Bible that leadership is not reserved for just the few, as the Greek philosophers would have us believe. Greek philosophy will never be earth-ready or people-ready. The philosophy that is earth-ready and people-ready is the leadership philosophy of Jesus.

My understanding of human equality—my foundation and my rock upon which I stand—came from God. Moreover, the fact that all humans have the potential to lead gave me an appreciation for the intrinsic value of each life, while freeing me from the mental slavery transferred to me during the times of my ancestors' oppression. After reading the Bible, issues with racism became foreign to me; segregation and discrimination were resolved because I discovered that God is not a

God is a respecter of love, and love doesn't discriminate.

respecter of race, color, or social class. God is a respecter of love, and love doesn't discriminate.

Gifting of the Gods

So what's the big deal about Greek philosophers such as Plato, Aristotle, and Socrates? Why are their beliefs so different from the teachings of Jesus?

The Greek philosophers believed that leadership was not intrinsic or inborn, but rather it was divinely crowned and naturally endowed by birth traits given to a special few groups that the gods had chosen. As far as history is concerned, the Greeks were the first people to formalize theories about government and leadership.

When the Romans conquered the Greeks, they took their ideas of government and leadership and adopted it as their mantra. They became the most powerful and successful empire and ruled vast lands from Africa to London for more than two hundred years using their adopted Greek systems of philosophy and government.

The Roman Empire eventually disintegrated, but the philosophies that came from the Greeks remained intact, surviving and flourishing in Europe. The Europeans then took this philosophy and explored other worlds to colonize and expand their hegemony by using the Greek philosophy to dominate and enslave others. Today, this philosophy still exists, spreading damaging beliefs across the world, and perpetuating the cycle of slavery. Apparently, we haven't really learned from history—only replicated it.

I find it amazing that we want to reject religion in our schools and in everything that we do, and yet we want to talk about human rights and equality—with no true morality or belief system to uphold them. Slavery, Jim Crow Laws, the Holocaust,

Apartheid, and other forms of oppression and injustices have been the culmination of godless ideals that thrust mankind into anarchy. Why wouldn't we want to prevent these mindsets from prevailing again?

Today, we say we are so advanced, and yet we can't accept the fact that we were all born to be leaders. The more advanced we become, it seems the less equal we treat each other. Why wouldn't our institutions change their ideas about leadership, knowing that the ancient definition of *leadership* meant "the empowerment of certain unique traits and natural advantages that separate the few chosen from the rest of humanity"?

Over the years, writers and philosophers (as well as scientists) have used all forms of trickery to divide humans. Some used the color of skin to "prove" that some were better than others. Others defined intelligence by the size of one's cranium. The list goes on and on. So why wouldn't we want Jesus's philosophy of leadership to permeate our institutions if we *really* wanted to talk about equality? In fact, the closest we have come in America to equality is on our dollar bills. We put a slogan on each bill that says, "In God We Trust" (though we can't talk about Him in schools or federal buildings that are paid for with the very same money). And we proudly recite our national pledge, shamelessly admitting that our nation is united under one banner—by God—a God we can't talk about in public for fear of offending others.

The truth is, we don't really want equality. We superficially talk about it, but we deny the intrinsic value and worth of each individual. Keeping ourselves in a higher position by making others lower makes us feel important. Yet the teachings of Jesus amply demonstrate that *all are equal* and that *all have value*.

The Greek concepts of leadership are diametrically counter to everything that Jesus taught us. We need to rethink this philosophy of leadership and rediscover the original leadership philosophy established by the Creator Himself if we are to become the leaders we were all meant to be. We need to accept the fact that leadership is not this impenetrable, ill-defined, godlike feature that "the gods" have given to only the elite few. Instead, leadership is inherent and intrinsic in all of us.

A god who gives others special gifts to rule, dominate, enslave, oppress, and subjugate others is a god I am not interested in. Sadly, this is the kind of god that we have elevated in many of our institutions. We have accepted a god, presented by the Greeks, who devalues people.

We have to reject the Greek god and accept the one true God who created everybody to dominate, rule, lead, and exercise authority over the earth—and never over people.

God Has Already Called You

Not too long ago, I was facilitating a mastermind group study for high school students looking to grow in their leadership, and during one of the sessions, a question came up that I believe many people are quietly asking. A girl in the group asked, "Can you give me clarity on leadership? You said that every human on earth—regardless of their race, color, education, and socioeconomic status—is a leader and a dominator. But if we are all leaders and not meant to have dominion over people, what do we lead and what's our leadership over?" In other words, her question was, "If everyone was born to lead, who will follow?" Perhaps as you read this book, you've been thinking the same way. That's a legitimate question. But it also proves that you have been perfectly brainwashed by the Greeks who believed that we needed to have leaders and followers, right? Wrong!

I told the group, "You were created to lead and to dominate in a domain of gifting, and never to dominate humans. When you lead and dominate in your gifted domain, people will be attracted to you. Your goal in life, therefore, is never to focus on pursuing people to follow you, but to focus on discovering yourself—your gift."

Let me simplify this concept in three principles:

1. You were born to dominate and lead, but never over people.
2. You were born to dominate and lead in a domain of gifting.
3. The discovery of your gift births your leadership and greatness.

Every human on earth, male or female, black or white, rich or poor has been crowned and endowed with the power and authority to have dominion over everything that moves on the surface of the earth, except humans. Mankind is off limits. Yet the thought that everybody is a leader is one of the most difficult concepts for us to understand. Our culture tells us that to be a leader, you need followers. And we're not the only ones who have it wrong. In fact, the Chinese have a proverb that enforces this misconception about leadership: "He who thinketh he leadeth and has no one following him is only taking a walk."

Dominion denotes to rule, to be king, to control, to govern, to lead, to manage, to master, and to keep creating. Dominion was and still is the mandate and assignment that was given to both men and women, and within that mandate lies each of our unique purposes and gifts of leadership. In other words, God gave us government, kingship, leadership, rulership, management, stewardship, and authority over five kingdoms and humans were not part of these kingdoms. This is emphatically stated in the early chapters of Genesis:[10]

Let us make mankind in our image, in our likeness, so that they may rule over the fish in the sea and the birds in the sky, over the livestock and all the wild animals, and over all the creatures that move along the ground.

When I discovered the true mandate for leadership, my whole world changed. I realized that I was listening to other people's ideas and concepts of leadership, instead of the Creator's.

You Came from Royalty

Defining *leadership* has been an elusive and nebulous dream for thousands of years. True leadership is a thing of beauty. You know it when you see it, but you cannot even define it. You can study a million people to see what made them great, and you can use all kinds of assessment tools and complicated formulas, but when you really want to define something elusive like *greatness* or *leadership*, you look for consistency. In other words, when you meet somebody who is outstanding and effective, and that person makes an impact and changes history, then you study him or her for certain qualities and see if those qualities reoccur in other people who had the same results. That's how you define *leadership*.

For example, you may study Martin Luther King Jr., Nelson Mandela, Abraham Lincoln, Mother Teresa, Rosa Parks, and Moses or Joshua of the Bible. When you begin to study these different characters, you begin to see consistent qualities in each individual that made them successful leaders in their assignments. Therefore, you define *leadership* based on certain qualities.

The origin of true leadership finds its roots in the Bible—a true story about a King, a Kingdom, and the royal family. We are told that God created the heavens and then the physical, material earth. God's original intent for creating the physical earth is to extend and colonize the visible planet with the invisible Kingdom of heaven. He would accomplish this perfect idea through

His apex of creation so they can have leadership and rulership and build kingdoms on the earth to reflect the invisible realm through their influence under Him. This makes us heirs to the Kingdom—royalty on earth.

I was born into a country that was once a colony called the Gold Coast and under the kingdom of Great Britain. Her majesty, the Queen of Britain, and her family were all royalty. When they colonized Ghana, instead of extending that royalty to all of us, they restricted the royalty to just themselves, and they considered our ancestors to be their subjects. But a true kingdom doesn't have subjects.

God's Kingdom is different and supersedes all other kingdoms, because, in His Kingdom, all citizens are royalty and are part of the royal family of God. Rome was the first city to copy the idea of the kingdom—God's original idea of colonization—but the extension of their influence ended up oppressing, enslaving, and devaluing the people they colonized. Later when all the other European kingdoms came to Asia, Africa, the Caribbean, and the Americas to establish colonies, they made the natives subjects through forced labor.

Regardless of our personal histories and bloodlines, we are all royalty in God's eyes. Still, many are acting as subjects because they are still suffering from the past oppression that was inflicted on their ancestors and was generationally passed along to them through cultural and family ties. We need a change of mind to inherit our true identity as royalty again!

Jesus has made the way possible for us, and today, through Him, I know my origin. I have meaning in my life. I know my identity. I know my potential. I know how to differentiate between good and evil, and I know my destiny. Do you know who you are, where you come from, why you are here, what you can do, and where you are going? You have to answer these questions too before your gift can be fulfilled on earth.

God's idea of Kingdom colonization is a penetration of love, grace, goodness, and fellowship with one another. The mandate of dominion can be carried out effectively when we all discover the domain that has been given to us to rule.

How does the mandate to have dominion over the planet transpire into our leadership? I believe that to effectively carry out the mandate, we must first discover our particular domain or area that we were born to exercise rulership over.

Since we are all children of God, we have all been given a gift to impact our environment around us, in the realm of our dominion mandate. Dominion is all about revealing your gift. Your gift makes you successful, makes you great, and makes room for you. It takes a Kingdom of leaders, kings, and rulers—not just one leader and millions of mindless followers.

God Chooses the Imperfect

History is replete with great leaders who changed the course of history and whose lives defied the traditional concepts of the times. Many biblical characters and historical characters were considered outcasts, not deemed to do great things; they were rejected and condemned by fellow humans. Yet they rose to greatness. They became pillars in their communities and examples to the world. Anyone who has read a little about such memorable champions as Moses, Gideon, Joshua, Naomi, David, Joseph, and countless others will agree that their humility catapulted them to greatness.

Let's take Moses, for example. If he had lived among the Greeks, he would have been considered an outcast. Exodus 4 is a powerful scripture that shows why: Moses didn't possess the rhetoric or the art of speaking in front of people. He had a speech impediment. He stammered. In fact, because of this defect, he tried to resist God's call on His life.

Moses tried to give excuses by telling God that he wasn't a charismatic speaker like the Egyptians would want, and that he was slow in speech. Of course, God knew all of this already.

The response God gave him was profound. He said to Moses, "Who made men lame; who made men tame? Is it not I?" God didn't heal Moses of his speaking disability. His inability to speak coherently had nothing to do with his innate leadership potential. Now, if the Greeks had their way with Moses, he would have never been allowed to become a speaker, and he would have never reached his potential and discovered his leadership ability.

Instead, God equipped Moses to be a leader in spite of his disability. In fact, because of Moses's defect, his brother Aaron's purpose came alive! Now we see why the story of Moses defies all the collective leadership ideas given by the Greeks.

Servant leadership is critical because it reveals the intrinsic value that each of us have and the appreciation that we need to give to each other. Trying to do everything by yourself actually means you are restricting others from fulfilling their purposes.

Your defect is somebody's purpose; your weakness is somebody's strength. If we were all born perfect, then we wouldn't need anybody's help for anything. Whatever you are weak at is another person's purpose. Don't deprive them of that opportunity to lead in their gift!

Remember that leadership has nothing to do with your personality. This is why we have so many failed leaders in the world. People are following personalities, and when they get bored, they follow someone else. Even with a disability, Moses became one of the greatest leaders who ever lived—and history can never forget him.

The Leadership Philosophy of *Giftocracy*

In the world of the historical Greeks and in our world today, not everybody is seen as a leader. But in God's Kingdom, everybody is born a leader—and, placed within humans, are leadership roles.

You are a leader, and God created you to lead in an area of gifting. Your leadership is manifested when you serve your gift to the world. The greatest among you will be the servant of all—therein lies the heart of Jesus's servant-leadership philosophy and the philosophy of *Giftocracy*.

My philosophy is one that is built on the biblical tenants that:

1. ***God created every human being on earth to be a leader and to manifest his greatness.***
We all have leadership and greatness trapped within us. I use the word *trapped* because unfortunately, most people will die having never discovered their gifts or having met their true selves.

   Our culture, education system, and environments don't automatically make room for us to meet our true selves. So even though we have leadership and greatness residing within us, whether that leader emerges and becomes activated and fulfills our assignment on earth depends several factors: the environment that we place ourselves in, the information that we expose ourselves to, the belief systems that we cultivate, and our ability to activate ourselves by that information.

2. ***You were born to lead, but you must become a leader.***
The best way to unpack this is to use the familiar concept of a seed. A seed was created to become a tree, but it must

go through a process to become that tree. The process has to do with three things:

1. It has to be placed in the right environment.
2. It must receive the right nutrients.
3. It needs time.

These three principles are also necessary for every human to become what they were born to be. First, as we've discussed, you need the right environment. Second, you need nutrients, which I call *knowledge*. Third, you need time. It takes time to go through the process of discovering, developing, becoming, and manifesting your true self. But notice the first one is the most important. The principle of environment is the key to life.

3. You possess the potential and the capacity to lead.
You possess the ability, but that doesn't mean you automatically will embrace it. The word *potential* means having the power or ability to do something, but which has not been manifested yet. *Capacity* means that you possess the capability to do something, but you've never exercised that capability.

This is also true of a person. You have the potential to lead, but whether you express and manifest that ability is another thing. My belief is that trapped inside of you is an untapped person that we have never met—yet.

4. You were created to lead in a domain of gifting.
True leadership and true greatness have very little to do with ruling people or leading people, and more to do with serving people through your gift. I know that this philosophical statement becomes challenging for people

to understand, because as we've discussed earlier, most people don't even know what gift they have.

Still, no human came to earth without a gift. Nobody came to earth empty. Everyone came with something—some gift—that humanity needs. In other words, you were sent to earth to serve your gift to humanity. When you discover your gift, you have discovered your value. You become valuable when you discover what you are meant to serve to humanity.

5. *True leadership—true greatness—is self-discovery.*
People who aspire to become leaders rarely become leaders because they think leadership is something you learn, study, some techniques you become skilled in, or some principles you apply to controlling and managing situations or people. That's why they never become true leaders. True leaders never try to be leaders.

History has produced what I call *hesitant* leaders. *Hesitant* means they were not interested in pursuing the leadership of others. They became leaders because their trapped potential was forced out by circumstances. In fact, they didn't know they were leaders until other people told them! True leadership is about discovering something about yourself that ignites you to serve humanity. This is why great leaders do not pursue or seek followers. Instead, they are ignited by a passion that gives them a sense of self. In turn, that gives them significance and value to other people.

I want to challenge you from this day forward to decide to meet yourself. To be yourself, you have to know yourself; and to know yourself, you have to know your source.

True leaders are those who never imitate others. They are authentic. To be authentic means you have discovered an originality about yourself, you love yourself, and you believe you are so valuable that you decide to humbly serve yourself to the world. That's when a true leader is born. Leadership, therefore, has very little to do with doing something and more to do with becoming something—becoming yourself.

You may think, "Sure, but does my one little gift matter in the big scheme of things? After all…there are seven billion people." The answer is yes! Even with seven billion of us alive today, all the billions who have died, and the billions who are yet to be born—all have a prepared position that belongs to them. Your leadership position—*your greatness*—*belongs to you*; yours does not belong to your neighbor, your grandfather, or your boss. In the entire span of humanity, no matter how crowded you might think the world is, no one else can take your place—your prepared position.

Your fingerprint is different from the fingerprints of every one of the billions of people on this earth. Since you are truly one of a kind, you might as well learn to become comfortable in your own skin.

Declare independence from all competitions, all fears, and all scarcity mind-sets. Instead of wasting your time competing with others for positions of prestige, power, and leadership, spend your time nurturing your gift and sharing it with others.

PART THREE

Give:
The Meaning of Life is to
Give Your Gift Away

CHAPTER NINE

DEVELOPING A GAME PLAN
FOR LIFE

"A good plan is like a road map; it shows the final
destination and usually the best way to get there."
—Stanley H. Judd

Have you ever met a prisoner who planned to be in prison?
I have been to prison a few times to visit a friend who was
convicted, and I noticed that during conversations with several
of the inmates, none of them told me they planned to be there.
So prison is filled with people who either didn't have a plan, or
they had a bad plan!

Another group of people who often seem not to have a plan
are athletes and entertainers. The famous boxer Mike Tyson
made three hundred million dollars during his career—yet today,
he's broke. How do you make that amount of money and end up
broke? It's the same thing that happens to people who win the
lottery and wind up broke a few years later. It happens to people
who get promotions, raises, and inheritances—the minute they
have more money, instead of pausing and making a plan for

how to manage it responsibly, they blow it on material things, vacations, friends, and partying. Then when the money runs out, they're left broke and alone.

When you don't have a plan for your life, your money, and your time, you can be sure that somebody else does. Your friend does, your agent does, your promoter does, or your parents do. This particular boxer owned twenty-two cars and seventeen homes. He clearly didn't seem to have a plan other than to spend it, so everybody else was happy to have a plan to receive his money! The car dealership had a lucrative plan for his money and the real estate agent also had a lucrative plan for his money. The only person who didn't have a lucrative plan for his own money was *him*.

In another unbelievable story, a football player who once had an eighty-million-dollar contract was on CNN after being arrested for selling drugs. When the interviewer asked why he was selling drugs, the former football player said he was broke and, in addition to being broke, he had fourteen children with twelve different women! See, he didn't have a plan for his life or his money.

As they say, when you fail to plan, you had better plan to fail.

So how do people end up in certain negative situations that they didn't dream about or anticipate? That answer is simple— they didn't have a plan. In life, everything of value, worth, or significance requires a plan. The more critical the event or project, the more essential the plan is. Since your life is important, your gift is necessary. Since your ability to fulfill your purpose is critical, you'd better have a plan.

> **If you don't have daily objectives for your life, you qualify as a dreamer.**
> —Zig Ziglar

A Planning Epiphany

My planning epiphany occurred when my best friend and business partner, Waid, and I got the opportunity of a lifetime to fly our first plane. I was especially interested in an instrument called the "Attitude Indicator," and wanted to know more about it.

Before we even got on the plane, Tom, the owner, took a clipboard and said, "Guys, this is what happens prior to a flight." He went on to say that every pilot has to have a flight plan before they are allowed to take off.

Because I was not a licensed pilot and didn't know anything about planes, Tom took the clipboard and started talking to himself. He would mention an instrument in the plane, and then he'd say out loud to himself, "Check." One by one he called out every instrument and every item on his list and responded: "Check."

When I saw he was nearly finished with the list, I asked him, "Do you do that before every flight?"

He said, "Just a minute, Michael." He made sure he did all of his checks first before answering me. Then he said, "We cannot take off without doing that because this plane has humans on board, and humans are the most valuable cargo, and you cannot take off by guessing."

We couldn't leave the ground without a flight plan. The tower will not clear a plane to leave unless a flight plan has been submitted and approved.

As I was sitting in the cockpit, strapped into the seat as if I were a copilot, I got the shock of my life when I realized how much planning is involved in flight. This was my great lesson on the value of planning that day.

Right before we took off, Tom said to us, "The tower knows that the plane is too important to be left to guessing or chance." We should adopt this same sentiment about our own lives!

When you look at yourself individually, think of yourself as cargo. You are too valuable, important, and significant to leave your life up to chance—so make a plan for where you want to go.

What Does the Flight Plan Include?

The flight plan, in addition to containing a very detailed checklist of items, includes the destination. In other words, you have to know where you are going before you can even take off. A pilot doesn't go to the airport and say, "I'm not exactly sure where we are going today. Let's just see what happens." Would you get on a flight if the pilot wasn't sure where he was going? No, you wouldn't. There has to be a clear destination.

The flight plan also requires information regarding the people onboard. You must tell the tower the exact number of people on board so that if something happens, they will know whom to contact. Another thing about the flight plan is that you have to determine what speed you're going to use and the altitude at which you're going to fly.

I also learned that when you are in the air, you don't fly in a straight line. There are basically roads or paths in the sky that are planned out in advance (because if there aren't any guidelines for the pilot to follow, planes will run into each other in midair!). Even if you want to change altitude for some reason, you have to get permission to change from the flight tower crew because there could be another plane near you that you can't see.

We can understand why the flight plan gives speed, altitude, and details of those on board; however, the flight plan also includes alternative routes. You have to have an alternative route before you leave the ground in case of bad weather; and you have to know which nearby airport to land at if something goes wrong.

The flight that day was a great experience. Seeing the earth from the windshield of a small plane, I was struck by the beauty of it all. I was also mentally comparing the many similarities between planning flights and planning our lives.

Planning Documents Vision

There should be things you write on paper—dreams, prayers, concerns, lists, plans, and vows—that should be only between you and your Higher Power. Other things should be shared with people so they can help you walk out your goals.

The only way to give unseen things substance is by writing them down, drawing them out, or speaking them aloud. People will not be impressed by how awesome your vision is if you don't have a plan on paper. If your vision is only in your mind—it exists only in your imagination. Once you put it down on paper, it becomes a tangible thing—your new reality—and you can make a plan to achieve it.

God desires our success more than you or I desire our own success. He commands us to establish the goals that lead us to our vision.

> **The ability to document the future is faith.**
> **To capture that which exists, but cannot be seen, is planning.**

You must stop, sit down, and make a plan if you are going to fulfill your vision. Success is the orderly ongoing advancement toward a goal. The ultimate achievement of that goal, the success, is arriving at the place where you have determined and planned to arrive—that is your *vision*.

Many people make beautiful plans, yet they do not follow through because of procrastination or laziness. So yes, you must plan your work. But then you have to work your plan daily.

Most people, myself sometimes included, don't always take the necessary time to sit down and think about our plans. If we take one action and see a little reward, we tend to coast along on cruise control until something changes. Yet we need to be proactive about planning and reevaluating each step along the way. If we spend no time on our dreams, no time on our vision, how can we expect to make them a reality?

Many of us are too busy making a living to find an exciting life worth living. But even in your current situation, you can make great strides by making a simple plan and taking the first step forward.

If you are on a job and want to get promoted, solve the next problem for your boss. Come up with an alternative plan to make things a bit better in your department. When you do this, your boss will keep an eye on you. A planner will always be promoted, because a planner is a visionary, a self-motivated person—and that's the kind of person who gets promoted.

Since we now know the principles for success—planning and hard work—we're off to a great start! Just make sure to keep your forward momentum as you go.

A Plan Is a Documented Desire

When we take the plans and desires in our heart and document them in writing—or when we draw them, paint them, or sing them—we will be amazed at how it attracts the right people and the right resources to us. This means the *plans* are your responsibility. All the intricacies of how that plan will happen? That's God's responsibility.

God knows that the plans we have seem impossible to us. Still, we shouldn't worry; just put all of it on paper and don't be afraid. After all, if you don't have any plans, He has nothing to direct.

If you know you're supposed to build a building, God says put the building on paper, along with all the dreams you have surrounding its purpose—even the financial details. Even if you need twenty million dollars to make it happen, just put the details on paper.

If God has told us *what* to do, *how* it's going to be done is none of our business. That's His responsibility.

This is such a relief when we truly understand this concept, obey it, and apply it to everything we do. It takes away all the stress and the worrying about money and how our dreams and visions will be fulfilled when the only thing we are to do is write our vision down.

> **To man belongs the plans of his heart, but to God belongs the answer of the tongue.**[11]

We should not be afraid of how much it's going to cost. And this is serious because some of us are dreaming some very large and expensive dreams! It can be frustrating being stressed about how it's going to be paid for. But just put it on paper and watch Him move.

So what is it that you see that won't leave you alone? What is that vision you've had since you were a child that still runs circles in your head? When will you accept your vision of a building, a sports field, a yoga studio, or a worship and teaching room? Whatever it is that you are dreaming of, write it down—all of it—and be amazed at how quickly the pieces fall into place.

> **If you want the Lord to lead you, attract Him. We have to make a plan that attracts God.**

Adapting to Time and Change: The Secrets to Success in Life

Two of the most important and powerful forces on earth are time and change. These are the only two things that are guaranteed in life. (Even death and taxes fall under "time and change!")

Time and change are no respecter of persons. Everybody has to deal with these two factors. We must discover how we handle both of them, because our reactions will determine how we live our lives.

The key to Kingdom success on earth is initiating and planning change—instead of always reacting to change that someone else has initiated. To be honest, change will happen with or without you; and time will move on regardless of your cooperation. Since we can't control these two elements, they must be *managed* instead, through planning and execution.

It might sound like a big task, but success is always in your hands. Think about it: Everybody has to manage time and change. When you wake up every morning and you still have breath in you, you are experiencing time and change, irrespective of your age, social class, or finances. Change happens to everyone, so if you want to benefit from it instead of suffer under it, make a plan to make the best of the time you have, and the most of the changes that occur in your life.

Your dream is only a dream until it has a plan. Below are some easy reminders of why a plan is so important to our daily lives:

1. The secret to success in life is effective management of time and change.
2. The principle key of managing time and change is planning.
3. Planning is the most important principle of success in life.

4. The only regulator of time and change is planning. Without a plan, time and change will ruin your life.

People are destroying their lives by living recklessly without a plan, or they are miserable because they didn't get the kind of life they wanted. They'll often say that they didn't have enough time or the right opportunities. But we all have the same twenty-four hours in a day. You were created to live life, and not for life to live you. The only way for you to live life and be in control of your destiny is through time management.

God has the capacity to plan and so do humans. This makes you different from a dog or a monkey, a cow or a bird. These animals don't plan. They live by instincts, and their actions are repetitive each day. They live to eat, mate, and die. If we were honest, some of our lives sound a little too close to this.

Stanley H. Judd said, "A good plan is like a road map; it shows the final destination and usually the best way to get there." If you've ever been on a road trip, you know that it is easier to change a plan than to not have a plan in the first place. A plan doesn't just show you where you want to go, but it also shows you (usually) the best way to get there. It can also save you time.

Up ahead, there will be many roads to get to your destination—your purpose. When you meet an obstacle in life, it doesn't mean you should stop and turn back. It simply means you should recalculate and navigate around the obstacle to keep moving forward.

If you have just enrolled in school but find out you're pregnant, don't quit school or abort the baby. Recalculate your options and continue to move forward, even if it takes a little longer to finish school.

If you've lost a job, or had a major health issue, don't panic or do anything drastic. Instead, recalculate. Take a step back so you can view your options and then proceed to navigate around the obstacle. When life happens—and it will surprise us from time to time—don't give up on your dreams. Go another route. Take advantage of other options. Reinvent your future with a new plan. You become what you plan for your life.

Gordon B. Hinckley made this profound statement: "You can't plow a field simply by turning it over in your mind." We know this to be true. There are people in each of our lives who have been thinking for ten, twenty, or thirty years about what they would *like to do*, but they never do it. They just keep thinking about it. One day, they meet someone who is doing the very thing they were thinking of doing and instead of becoming inspired to finish, they become even more discouraged because someone else beat them to it and did what they wanted to do.

Don't get discouraged. Stop *thinking* and start doing—by making a plan. Turn your thoughts into a design. Stop procrastinating now. Stop telling people you are going to do something; just do it and show them what you did. Just like the athletes who had money and spent it all, if you don't design your life—if you don't have a plan for your business, your marriage, or your future—somebody else will.

Planning without action is futile. Action without planning is fatal.

The moment you emerged from your mother's womb, your journey began. Make sure you make the most of your time and your talents before the journey ends. And understand that sometimes your journey will take you both to and through unfamiliar places. Learn to enjoy the ride wherever it takes you.

And remember, it's never too late—or too early—to start planning for the future.

Moving from the Familiar to the Unfamiliar

There came a point in my life when everybody around me was used to what I did. They knew me as Michael the soccer player. They were familiar with that title because that's what brought me to the US for high school, college, and eventually allowed me to play at the professional level. My family back in Ghana only knew that it was the familiarity of soccer that allowed me to make money to support them. But when I discovered the totality of who God created me to be and decided to step into it—which meant ending my professional soccer career—everybody around me, including my family, became my enemy. My family especially couldn't understand why I gave up soccer, because, to them, that's the only thing I knew how to do and the only thing that allowed me to send money to support them. They were so used to that comfort that when I stepped into the unfamiliar, they stopped talking to me for several weeks.

I am here to tell you that the only way for you to maximize your true potential is by letting go of the familiar and stepping into the unfamiliar, even when it severs or distances some relationships. People around you will try to discourage you, criticize you, and even become your enemy when you step into the unfamiliar. But if you are radical enough to make that decision to step into it anyway, your life will never be the same. The unfamiliar, while uncomfortable territory, really is your friend. Stepping into the unfamiliar will change your life and bring you into a new realm of existence.

All around us, people are dying inside because they are surrounded by people who do not challenge them, motivate them, or move them forward. They look like you, dress like you, think like you, and act like you. The group mentality thinks that in order for everybody to be accepted, we must wear the same stuff and feel the same way. Everybody has to fit in a little box. But what do you do when you are stuck in a box and you have a problem? Your potential can never be realized as long as you stay in the box. Still, the majority of people will stay in the box at the expense of minimizing their potential—because it is comfortable, or at least, familiar.

But you can never move to a new dimension of anointing, a new level of maturity, and new heights until you are willing to leave the familiar.

You can never move to a new level of maturity and new heights until you are willing to leave the familiar.

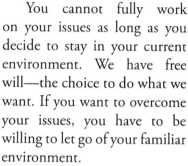

You cannot fully work on your issues as long as you decide to stay in your current environment. We have free will—the choice to do what we want. If you want to overcome your issues, you have to be willing to let go of your familiar environment.

Sometimes you will be taken to places that are unorthodox, untried, and unseen. The methods and plans God uses change with each situation. Many times, you will have to get away from everybody you know and everybody you are used to, and get to a new place to work on yourself. If you are no longer surrounded by the voices of others, you can more clearly hear His voice—the only one that matters.

I believe changes occur with a simple principle: How badly do you want it? Do you want what God has for you badly enough to come out of your comfort zone, the status quo, in order to get what you need? Or are you playing hard to get, insisting that God has to come into your environment and conveniently bless you? I want people to come to a point in their lives that they can say, "Whatever it takes, at all costs, I will do what it takes to get what I need from God."

When I made the choice to step away from soccer, I knew I would have to disassociate myself from my friends and family who didn't understand or agree. If living my dream means going through some pain or separating myself from people who are holding me back from the next move of the call of God in my life, so be it. If achieving my vision means going through division, leaving the familiar, my comfort zone, security—I will do it. If it means leaving my best friends, my parents—it is worth it. If it means living with people who don't look like me, reading books that I have never read before, or being in a new environment, I am ready to go on a trip with God because I want to get everything that He has for me! Whatever the cost, whatever the price, I am willing to pay it. I pray you are also ready to step into the unknown for the blessings waiting there for you.

Six Principles of Planning

Dreams are successions of images, ideas, emotions, and sensations that occur subconsciously or involuntarily (meaning, without your help) in the mind during certain stages of sleep. We also think of dreams as the ideal life we wish we had. Though our dreams may be real and within our reach, our plans give them breathe and life. Just dreaming is not enough. Your dream is waiting for a *plan*.

In order to create a solid plan, here are six principles that will help you visualize your dream, expand your vision, and give it parameters as you put it on paper:

1. *Get the Vision:* Jesus said if you want to build a tower, you have to have a clear image of your destiny, a clear vision of where you want to go. In other words, first you must get the vision. Don't start until you know where you are going.

2. *Sit Down:* Sitting down means pausing and taking a break from your hectic schedule. Go somewhere you can think, mediate, and get away from the noise. Lock yourself in

the closet if you have to! Get away from your family, your children, and your friends, and get God's ideas.

3. **Estimate:** This requires you to focus. *Estimating* means using your imagination to see the projects you want to accomplish. Assess things to see what could happen. Do an analysis of your strengths and your weaknesses, as well as an analysis of what it's going to take to get things done.

4. **Count the Cost:** Cost includes price, impact, and demands. Everything you plan to do will cost you something. Think about the impact that it could have on your life and the life of your family. Consider the demands that it will make on you, and also the effort it may require of your energy, body, focus, time, and intellect. Cost may also mean identifying the friends and family members you might lose because of your vision.

   When I started One Kingdom Foundation, a nonprofit dedicated to building a leadership school in Ghana, many people (including my family back home and several of my host families in America) thought I had gone crazy to give up soccer, a game that I loved and played for twenty-three years. But I knew my mission was to build a leadership school to help restore self-image, self-esteem, and self-concept—and to empower, inspire, and transform the mind, body, and spirit of the youth in Ghana and beyond. My older brother didn't understand me; an American family that supported me when I was in college didn't understand me, either.

   What I didn't know then is that sometimes your destiny takes you away from certain things and interferes with any commitment you have. Also, sometimes your future may not keep you where you were born. Your vision, dream, or idea may cost you some relationships, even your family.

5. ***Commit It to God:*** God wants us to be specific when we ask for things. Don't ever give Him an open figure. When we say things like, "God bless me," He says, "With what?" God already knows exactly what you need; the benefit of saying it out loud or writing it down is for you—so that you can visualize something specific to work toward.

   Whatever you plan to do, whatever you need, give Him a cost. God will always exceed it for you. But He wants you to give Him the details for cost, maintenance, sustenance, and how the project is going to be furnished. If you give Him nothing, He has nothing to exceed.

6. ***Complete It:*** God wants you to start things and finish things; He wants you to feel the happiness that comes from completing your assignment. You should want to be like Jesus Christ who estimated the cost of dying on the cross and did it anyway. He was able to handle the pain and the stress because of the joy that was set before Him. Thankfully, your plans, no matter how big or difficult they may be, will likely be much less painful than Christ's death.

   You are stronger than you think. Let your determination carry you forward to complete the task you've set out to do.

Your Personal Plan

Now that you've read about the necessary steps needed to create an effective plan, I want you to do this exercise for yourself. Pick up a blank sheet of paper, isolate yourself, and sit down with God. On your blank sheet of paper, I want you to write down what's on your mind, following the previous steps 1–5.

Plan your upcoming year in detail, according to your vision. Allow your dreams and passions to create your plans. Then begin working step number 6 and initiate and expect major changes in your life. Don't allow life to catch you by surprise. Commit now to making changes that will guide the destiny of your life. This might mean giving up certain foods that you regularly eat, leaving a job you're unhappy in, or ending relationships that can't help you. You may need to break some habits that will affect your destiny. But you are more than able to do this!

Once you have developed a solid game plan for your life (and no, this doesn't mean you'll know *every detail* or have *every answer*), pray daily for the rest of this year for guidance from God. Keep giving your dreams and concerns to Him! Continue to update your list and your plans. God will take your plan and run with it.

> **If every single thing had to be considered before we begin, nothing would ever begin.**
>
> —Unknown

CHAPTER TEN

PASSING IT ON:
LEGACY MATTERS

"A leader's lasting value is measured by succession."
—John C. Maxwell

Have you thought about the legacy you are leaving behind? If I were a stranger at your funeral, would I be inspired by the life you lived? What would your friends and family have to say about the goals you accomplished and the people you impacted along the way?

Everyone has asked themselves these thought-provoking questions from time to time. If you are an aspiring leader (and you are), it is even more important to examine these questions as the issue of legacy serves as the foundation and structure from which long-lasting footprints are created.

It is important to recognize where we are in relation to the goals we want to achieve. Knowing our position as early as possible is the key to setting obtainable expectations for ourselves and for those who work with us and live with us.

Celebrating the Next Generation

Last year, I was invited by Charlie Vantramp, the former director of the Miss Washington pageant show, to watch one of the Miss Washington's "Outstanding Teen" pageants. Every year, one teenager is crowned to represent the organization, and the winner holds the title of Miss Washington's "Outstanding Teen."

This title comes with an enormous responsibility. The title of Outstanding Teen affords the winner an opportunity to affect many people by allowing her a platform from which she can voice her passions, convictions, and overall mission in life. She becomes an instant role model and she must exhibit excellent behavior, communication skills, and values at all times over the next year.

Since I'm married to the former Miss Washington, Kristen Eddings, I was even more honored and privileged to attend the awards ceremony. It was a powerful and memorable moment, not just as a spouse, but as a human, because this event allowed me a glimpse into a world that shapes the lives of so many women spiritually, physically, and mentally. It made me even more proud of my wife when I saw what she had to go through to achieve the title. And it also taught me a valuable lesson about leadership.

As I looked around the room and felt the buzz of excitement, I could feel the weight and anticipation hanging in the air as families and event managers scurried about, making last-minute preparations and adjustments. From my vantage point, I could see these young ladies utilizing the same resourcefulness I had once used with my childhood friends while attempting to make our first soccer field. It seemed that every organizational and team-building skill was being utilized to its highest degree as the final minutes to show time grew near.

In many ways, the atmosphere at the pageant—hopeful and full of potential—reminded me of the soccer fields of my childhood. The settings were certainly different. I was now miles and years away from the little mud hut and dirt floors—but the spirit and the joy was the same.

The tradition of the Miss Washington's Outstanding Teen pageant commanded a reverence one could feel with every heartbeat. This community of women helping younger women was not focused solely on competition, but instead was a generational passing of the baton that focused on higher ideals and adherence to a structure that would yield promise, not only for the winner of the pageant, but also *for all who participated.* The parents of the young ladies who were participating weren't any different than the happy parents in my town of Ghana when provided with a platform from which their children could succeed.

We shuffled to our seats just as the show began. As the music grew louder, forty hopeful young ladies filled the stage and lit up the auditorium with a bright and fiery presence. In unison, they performed a dance that they had spent several days choreographing. Their fluid movement as a group was mesmerizing to watch. While each participant brought her own unique talent to the table, their efforts to move as one left a lasting imprint on my mind—it was the same teamwork I'd witnessed thousands of times on the soccer field.

As the event continued, each participant was measured by a certain amount of predetermined variables that would be assessed, calculated, and compared, in order to decide the grand pronouncement of Miss Washington's Outstanding Teen. The final variable would be a routine each young lady would present as a way of showcasing her defining talent. I'm not ashamed to admit that tears filled my eyes as I saw God's unique gifts in each of the contestants.

After the final individual routine, the crowd came to their feet in applause as the former Miss Washington's Outstanding Teen approached the crowd, singing and thanking everybody who had made her year so successful. Beaming with pride and purpose, she went on to express her experience as Miss Washington's Outstanding Teen and the leadership lessons she learned along the way. Discovering what roles she was not particularly good at was the most important lesson she learned. As she grew, she got better at delegating those tasks to individuals with those particular talents.

This refreshingly humble spirit made it clear as to why she had won the year before. She expressed the importance of letting go of preconceived notions of leadership, and explained how becoming relatable, raw, and vulnerably human were the keys to her leadership success. While she would be passing on the title of Miss Washington's Outstanding Teen, she would be doing so with a new future of achievement in mind that would not have been possible without her experience in the role.

In her final moments with the title, she expressed her excitement at sharing these lessons with the new Miss Washington's Outstanding Teen, and reminded the crowd of the importance each generation has on the next.

Giving up our leadership crown doesn't mean we lose our crown.

After the event, still in awe of the powerful lessons I had just witnessed through our nation's youth, I reflected on the transition of a legacy that occurred right before my very eyes. It served as one of the greatest leadership principles I have ever learned. It taught me that as a leader, we should never fear giving up our leadership crown, title, or position to the next generation. And we should never fail to mentor, train, and encourage those who come behind us.

Prior to this reflection, I had looked at the idea of pageants and games largely as those events that simply produced winners and losers. Of course, the game of soccer meant more to me than that, but it wasn't until this event that I so clearly witnessed the true nature of our human need to pass along our leadership and legacy-building skills.

Most of the time, we fail to mentor people. We fail to give up leadership. We fail to train and to transfer leadership to the next generation because we think that giving up our leadership means we are going to be forgotten. Not only is that sentiment incorrect, but it is also incredibly selfish to keep our gifts to ourselves.

Let this be a reminder: We should never be afraid to pass along our leadership because doing so would be robbing other generations of *their leaders*.

Define Your Life in One Sentence

In our leadership pursuit, many people are living as if they will never die. But I'll just state the obvious: *everybody dies*. Being conscious of the truth that we have limited time on earth will help us to maximize our days, months, and years.

As a little boy growing up in Ghana, I remember my mother saying to me, "Son, don't live life as though you will never die." I didn't understand what that meant back then, but I fully know now what my mother was impressing on me. She was helping me catch what I call the "spirit of legacy."

My mother's words always helped me stay motivated about becoming the best version of myself and maximizing every opportunity, desire, and goal in my heart. However, it's fair to say that the goals and desires for my life have been altered quite a bit. Over the years, I have changed my goals and these changes have set me on a path to tapping more into my leadership potential.

Several years ago, while reading John C. Maxwell's *The 21 Irrefutable Laws of Leadership*, I came across the concept known as a "life sentence," an idea that was first introduced by writer Clare Boothe Luce. The life sentence describes the purpose of one's life or goal. Clare believes that a great leader gets one sentence. This has been evident in my own life.

For example, my first life sentence as a boy in Ghana was "to become a great soccer player." Years later, when I was recruited by the soccer academy, my sentence changed to: "I want to be the best goalkeeper."

For more than half a decade at the academy, I worked hard as a goalkeeper, winning tournaments and games with my team. I did so well as a goalkeeper that I was the first player in the academy to train with our local professional team. However, when I received a scholarship to come to the United States to further my education and continue to play the game I loved, I realized that the only way to go to college was through a scholarship, not as a goalkeeper, but as a field player. That's when I decided on my next life sentence: "I want to be the best field soccer player."

After three years of hard work and multiple training sessions with my friends, I was awarded a soccer scholarship to the University of California Santa Barbara, and then eventually played on the professional level for the Seattle Sounders.

When I got to the professional level, many people were inspired by my story; but when I got to Seattle, my focus changed again soon after the end of my first season with the team. That's when I chose my current life sentence, which is: "I want to inspire leaders to inspire leadership in others." I wake up every day ready and excited to equip, inspire, and empower individuals, companies, churches, and organizations to inspire others.

I have found on my journey that, at each stage, I have experienced incredible maturity and growth, and my understanding of the world has enlarged. On my twenty-sixth birthday, I reflected on my previous sentences and saw a unique sequence—a common denominator—of all the changes I embraced. In other words, inspiring others has been the foundation of my heart's desires, no matter what I was doing. I became a good goalkeeper, a good soccer player, and I'm working to become a great inspirational leader so that I can inspire others to do more and to make a difference in the world.

As I continue to grow on my journey to inspiring others, I am realizing that my "life sentence" is what I will be known for when I lie on my deathbed. At my funeral, I hope people will say things like, "Michael is the guy who inspired me to meet myself, who convicted me to discover why God put me on this planet, and who inspired me to never give up on my dreams." I hope that, at my funeral, there will never be any guessing of the legacy I left behind.

It isn't morbid to think about what others will say when you're gone. It's important! What do you want your friends and family to say about you? If you don't like what comes to mind, you can start changing your path today so you can become the person you want to be.

As you think about your legacy, know that it—along with a good sentence—carries a clear message, a single message that doesn't only indicate the legacy *you leave*, but also charts the direction of your life.

When we look back on the lives of great men and women, we see that they were all struck by a single goal. All of their lives were punctuated by one desire, one passion that totally consumed them. When we allow our lives to stand for a single purpose, it takes on a more powerful stance.

We all have that one thing inside of us, screaming to get out. Unfortunately, we allow ourselves to get confused and turned around by things that are less important to us. Then we use those same obstacles as excuses as to why we don't accomplish greater things. The interesting thing is that when we take the road to accomplishing those great things, as difficult as it may be, we start to see these less-important things for what they are, and we can focus more clearly on what truly matters.

Remember what Clare Boothe Luce said: "A great man is a sentence." What is your life sentence?

Being Humble Is Honorable

One of the most misunderstood and confused words in the English language is the word *humility*. The etymology of *humility* comes from the Latin word *humus*, which denotes soil, especially rich, organic dark soil. A seed planted in rich fertile soil will transform into abundance. The mustard seed becomes a tree with more seeds. Now if you've ever seen a mustard seed, it looks like a speck of sand, but when it grows, it becomes a bounteous harvest.

Everything begins by nurturing the soil—the humus. In other words, when we have an abundance of humus (humility) in our own lives, we develop, we grow, we expand, and we nurture others around us to grow.

When we think about this word, we may visualize being passive, slumping our shoulders, or being subservient or submissive. This is far from the truth. Humility has more to do with self-discovery, self-acceptance, growing, and learning. It implies a continual acceptance of who you were created to be. It's not about being submissive, but about living life abundantly with our heads up, shoulders back, as we expand ourselves and express our fullest selves, and then empower others to do the same. Then the cycle begins again!

> **We cannot lead and influence others until we can influence and lead our *own lives*.**
> **We cannot impact and change the world until we have impacted and changed our own lives.**

The core connection between self-discovery, self-mastery, and leadership is what true humility is about. Empowerment, inspiration, and personal development enable us to lead others, because we cannot lead and influence others until we can influence and lead our *own lives*. We cannot impact and change the world until we have impacted and changed our own lives. Through humility, this process and transition will happen. Humility is a product of growth and development.

How to Develop Your Legacy[12]

In his bestselling book, *The 21 Irrefutable Laws of Leadership*, John C. Maxwell gives us four practical ideas to develop our leadership legacy that I've expanded upon. I believe that each individual is living a legacy every day, whether it's a good legacy or a bad one. The choice to be highly intentional about the kind of legacy we want to leave behind…is ours.

1. *Know the legacy you want to leave.*
   Knowing the kind of legacy you want to leave is the first step toward preserving a lasting legacy. As a leader, you have to be highly intentional about your life and make it a proactive one. In his book, *Training for Power and Leadership*, author Grenville Kleiser makes this remark:

> Your life is a book. The title page is your name, the preface your introduction to the world. The pages are a daily record of your efforts, trials, pleasures, discouragements, and achievements. Day by day, your thoughts and acts are being inscribed in your book of life. Hour by hour, the record is being made that must stand for all time. Once the word *finis* must be written, let it then be said of your book that it is a record of noble purpose, generous service, and work well done.

Our lives are being documented every day; therefore, knowing the legacy we want to leave behind helps us to stay focused on what we're doing so that our goals are in line with that legacy. Without defining what kind of legacy we want to leave, we are at risk of giving energy to activities that will delay our purpose.

Planning the legacies we are leaving behind forces introspection and will inspire us to dig deeper into our culture, families, and communities. The defining of one's legacy will ultimately connect us with those whose lives we intend to touch.

When defining our legacy, think about whose life you want to touch, why, and how. If you can explain your intended legacy in one sentence, you are on the right track!

2. *Live the legacy you want to leave.*

We cannot leave behind what we don't already have. We cannot expect others to uphold a legacy that we don't already possess within ourselves. We can't lead others until we can lead ourselves. Our effectiveness at interpersonal leadership will be determined by the quality of our personal relationships and is a function of our "doing," and not solely on our ability to talk about it. Regardless of what you've been taught, there is no such thing as, "Do as I say, and not as I do."

> **No written word nor spoken plea can teach our youth what they should be, nor all the books on all shelves. It's what the teachers are themselves.**
> —John Wooden (Coach, UCLA Men's Basketball)

One of the greatest decisions I made when my leadership journey began was that I would never teach anything that I wasn't willing to endorse in my own life and in my own behaviors. As you think about your legacy, you may want to revisit some of your own behaviors, so that your actions more accurately align with your words.

3. *Choose who will carry on your legacy.*

As I stated earlier, the only guarantee in life is death—well... death, time, change, and taxes, to be exact. While it might seem morbid or extreme to plan a legacy around our demise, the temporary nature of our lives is an important thing to consider when determining how our legacies will carry on in our absence. This question should instigate a closer look at the type of legacy we want to leave and how that legacy will translate to future generations.

When I began my journey in studying the character of Jesus, one of the first things I discovered about His life was that, during His short time on earth, He never built a single building. For most of us, in our materialistic, leadership thinking, we believe that if we build monuments, structures, or skyscrapers, those things will become our legacy. Yet, I remember a trip I made where I witnessed a city collapse as a result of a tsunami. Buildings, bridges, and other structures that had taken years to build were decimated in the blink of an eye. Coming home from that trip, I experienced a new awakening and higher level of awareness that our legacies should never be focused on buildings or things that are capable of being extinguished by fickle conditions like the weather.

Rather than building big buildings with names on them, God focused on building structures *within people*. He understood that people will always outlast buildings. This is why, during Jesus's work on earth, He focused on selecting a few groups of people and pouring His life into them. Therefore, the greatest investment you could ever make in life is in other people.

Even in my hometown, I was struck by how many leaders developed their legacies

> **All authority in heaven and on earth has been given to me. Therefore go and make disciples of all nations.**
> —Matthew 28:18-19

while under the oppression of colonialism. My country, formerly known as the Gold Coast, was colonized by Britain, a nation who considered my people second-class citizens in our own country. Similar to Apartheid, my people were not considered equal to those who had colonized and oppressed them.

One thing I discovered about the history of my people is that those who colonized and oppressed us *never* considered us to be leaders. In fact, they taught my ancestors how to be dependent on others. This is why many post-colonial countries continue to struggle with accepting power and empowering others. They don't know what to do with leadership, and that's why there is such an abuse of leadership in many of our nations.

As I pondered the statement made in Matthew 28:18–19, I wondered how my country's history related to my journey toward understanding the Bible. Most of the missionaries who came to our country didn't expect us to pose a challenge or to take over. Their predetermined expectation was that we would deem them superior and would look to them constantly and depend on them. Now here comes this man named Jesus, having all the power, empowering His people, and raising them up to continue work.

Most missionaries, oppressors, and colonizers that came to our country would have loved to have us worship them. Crucial, identifying information was hidden from us so that there was a spirit of praise around *them*. But not with Jesus. He came to teach us what His Father taught Him—what true leadership is all about. He possessed the ultimate "spirit of legacy."

People and their relationship with a higher calling are more important than buildings demanding credit. Jesus never left a building in His name. Instead, He left people who would speak of Him for eternity.

A true legacy is inextinguishable and lives on in the hearts and minds of people. My studies introduced me to many examples of this theory: Elijah focused on Elisha and gave him his cloak.

David focused on Solomon and gave him his crown. Moses focused on Joshua, Paul focused on Timothy, and Jesus focused on Peter.

So whom are we focusing on? Who are we training to take our place? Who are we coaching and mentoring to pass on the leadership crown?

4. *Make sure you pass the baton.*

Remember, the race is not for the swift, but for those who endure to the end. This is the mindset of many of our leaders today. They take pride in enduring to the end and risk losing everything they built because of their failure to train others. Recognizing when it is time to pass the baton is a crucial and defining step in *being* a leader.

Therefore, an effective leader is the one who leads with the next generation in mind. They make sure that they are inspiring rising leaders who will carry on their legacy long after they are gone. They provide opportunities for people to discover their unique gifts. They create an environment where those under them will have the opportunity to experience their goals.

True leaders are never threatened by up-and-coming leaders. In fact, a wise and effective leader will rejoice when those they counseled have a greater impact than they did.

A leader's lasting values is measured by succession.
—John C. Maxwell

The True Success in Succession

The first African leader who gave up power after the first term was Nelson Mandela. How can such a man (having been jailed for years, fighting for a cause, finally set free, and elected the first black president of his nation) not want reelection? That's unheard of in Africa.

Many historical and modern Africans who were supposed to give up power have tried to run again because they are addicted to the fame and wealth that position brings. But Mandela was the epitome of a leader with a true spirit of legacy. He understood that leadership is not about preserving power and possessing power, but about empowering people and mentoring them to serve.

I say to all African leaders (and any leader, for that matter): know when it's time to leave. Don't wait until people are tired of you to say good-bye or to be forced out of office. It's better to leave early than too late.

Mandela was beyond politics and understood that leadership is about preserving the next generation—not his own private ambitions within government. He understood that leadership is about principles, passion, values, people, and vision. He truly gave his life for the people.

Because of his selflessness, Mandela's life, along with that of many of the great leaders in history, has taught me something very important about leadership. It is my humble conclusion that we don't need more people in leadership. *We need more leadership in people.*

In Ghana, politics is the new way to gain wealth. People are flooding into politics because they know they can become rich from holding public office. But these people are not true leaders. They are there for their own private ambitions, and we should never confuse politicians with true leaders. We don't need more politicians in leadership. *We need more leadership in politicians.*

Mandela was not a politician. Even though he was smart and intelligent, he was beyond politics, deeper than politics. Politicians are more concerned about the next election and how they can stay in office, but true leaders are more concerned about how they can make a difference in their generation and the next, and about how they can better serve people.

Leadership is about *service*, not about being served. It is about *empowerment*, not having power over others. It's about *inspiration*, not manipulation. It's about *finding a purpose* that drives you to sacrifice for people, not about finding and maintaining followers. It's about *becoming something*, not about just doing something.

Mandela became the freedom he stood for. Even in jail, Mandela was still free because he understood that no human being can give another freedom. He was free from what people thought about him, free to follow his vision and claim his Giftocracy. He had a sense of generational obligation that all aspiring leaders should admire—leaders like you!

Another great leader, Dr. Martin Luther King Jr., gave the famous, "I Have a Dream" speech and encouraged African-Americans and other peace-minded individuals both in America and around the world to peacefully fight for equality. He was so dedicated to his message of peace—a legacy of equality—that he was willing to be beaten, threatened, and jailed; indeed, he died because of his ideas. And today the world is better because of his legacy.

Do you have the tenacity and courage to stand up for your beliefs in the face of adversity? What are you willing to sacrifice to ensure that your dreams, your gift, and your legacy is passed on to future generations? What about a few months of discomfort? What if it took a little longer…say, a few years of hard work? Would you move across the country, or even move to another country entirely if that's what it took? Would you be willing to give your life for your legacy?

As you think about your legacy of succession, you may look to the leaders you admire, your family, your heroes, and your cultural role models; but don't aspire to be like them or to copy them. You may desire to do great things—and you will accomplish them!—but do it from your own gifting, from your own dreams and passions.

You are the only *you* who has ever been and ever will be. Trapped inside of you is a powerful gift that only you can unwrap and unleash into the world through your actions.

It is your calling. Your purpose. Your destiny—this *Giftocracy.*

Let us dream big. May we never compromise. And let us continue to follow where the journey leads us, even into the great unknown.

Your future begins now—with a single step, a single word, a single choice.

Are you ready?

ONE KINGDOM FOUNDATION

When I was drafted by the Seattle Sounders Football Club and arrived in Seattle and I had a few goals in mind: My number-one goal was to work hard and do whatever I could to get on the field. My desire was to do well for the Sounders, play as many games as possible, and establish myself as one of the best rookie players in MLS. My second goal was to establish a nonprofit to help the youth in Ghana like myself who more often than not don't get the opportunity to realize their dreams. Giving back was very dear to my heart, since I had been provided with an opportunity to realize my dreams by the Right to Dream Academy.

I wanted to fulfill my soccer goals first—and then get busy volunteering and eventually starting my own nonprofit to inspire, empower, and equip young people both in Ghana and the US. But God had a different plan for my life. And to help me with that plan, He also gave me a new friend, Steve Zakuani.

Steve is a year older than me and had been in the league for two seasons before my arrival to Seattle. He was a gifted wide player (my favorite player to watch while in college), with great speed and smooth dribbling moves. He was the first teammate to approach me in the locker room and start a conversation by making fun of my hairstyle. (I think he was a little jealous of it.) He made me feel so welcomed, and as we talked and cracked jokes, it felt like we had known each other for years.

But it was our preseason training camp to Arizona that would change everything. We arrived in Arizona in the month of February, for a two-week preseason training that was beginning in March. Training sessions where fun and competitive, as both new and veteran players were fighting for a spot on the team. We ate dinner together as a team most nights, and all the new players had to introduce themselves and share something about their hopes and dreams. When it was my turn to introduce myself, I shared the vision that had always been in my heart. I told my teammates that ever since I was a little boy, my desire had been to play soccer professionally and to use that platform to start an organization that would build a school for young children in my village who don't get the opportunity to realize their dreams.

After dinner that night, we had a few hours to do whatever we wanted. I was a little tired, so I went back to my hotel room to lay my head down and read. That evening, Steve came to my room to hang out. During our conversation, he began sharing with me about his vision to build a sports academy back in the UK. We had deep discussions about leadership, purpose, vision, and how unique each individual is in life. He challenged me that night to think bigger, dream bigger, and never settle for less. He told me that I was born to make a difference and not just make a living. After he left my room, I couldn't go to sleep and stayed up a few hours after that, contemplating the many decisions and opportunities in life. Something had clicked inside me, and I knew I had to do something about it.

When we came back to Seattle after our preseason trip to Arizona, Steve Zakuani took me under his wing, mentored me, and introduced me to the life-changing works of Dr. Myles

Munroe. Through the direction and wisdom of both Steve and Dr. Munroe, I further discovered my true sense of significance and potential, and increased my awareness and oneness with God. I gained a new and deeper awareness of who I was created to be, which empowered me to transform and transcend the opinions and circumstances of my life. And some of the more unpleasant circumstances were right around the corner.

During practice one day, I pulled my hamstring. For the next three to four months, I could not participate in practice; and if you know anything about hamstring injuries, the slightest movements of running when it's not healed will reinjure it again. That's what happened to me. I reinjured my hamstring *three times* when I thought it was all healed. Instead of practicing, I spent months in rehab while watching my teammates practice. It was a very difficult period. I wanted to be out on the field—living my dream! Yet during my injury, I had time to think about my future and the dreams I wanted to fulfill outside of soccer.

When my hamstring injury was finally better and I was able to start practicing again, I was sent on loan to a lower division team in Florida called the Orlando City SC for a week to play for them and get myself game-fit. It was on this trip that I had the most vivid dream of my future destiny.

A little after midnight, after a long evening of practice with my new teammates, I came back to my room, ate dinner, and got in bed to read for a little while. As I lay there in bed, eyes wide open and staring at the ceiling, I saw clear pictures in my mind of what I was *really* born to do—and, to my surprise, it wasn't playing soccer on a lush green field in front of thousands. I saw pictures of a beautiful and familiar land. It was my village, and on the surrounding land were a few different buildings: a classroom, an auditorium, a dream room, a fitness center, dormitory, and faculty centers. I saw kids running around the campus with huge smiles on their faces. They were happy, healthy, and totally filled with joy!

As these pictures were being revealed to me, I heard an audible voice whispering into my ear, "Son, this is why I created you. You are to establish an organization that will create an environment where the youth can be inspired, equipped, and empowered to discover their purpose in life and maximize their true potential."

I was both afraid and excited at the same time! I was afraid because the vision that was revealed to me was too big—at least, that's what I thought at the time—and the voice was telling me to step away from soccer, *my dream*, for my life's new calling. At the same time, I was excited because the vision I saw appealed to a fulfillment of the deep calling I had always known was upon my life.

In that moment, I knew two things: First, I would open a school for children in Ghana. Second, my future in professional soccer was going to be a short one.

> **When you're operating in your gifting and purpose in life, two things happen: you become afraid and excited at the same time.**

When I came back to Seattle from Florida, equipped with a new vision, I no longer went out to bars with my teammates. Instead, I stayed in my room reading and learning everything I could that would prepare me for the next step. In fact, my roommates (Josh Ford and Servando Carrasco) during this process of transformation thought I was antisocial. They would ask me to go to dinner or a movie, and I would refuse because all I wanted to do was stay in my room and read. Before this, I'd never finished a book in my life, but now I was reading book after book, writing pages of notes for each one I read. Something was happening to me that I couldn't explain, but I loved every minute of this new journey.

I remember calling my best friend Waid Ibrahim and telling him that I was going to give up soccer to pursue this calling in my life—of course, he thought I was crazy. My wife Kristen Tetteh, who was then my girlfriend, also thought I was insane to leave soccer. Some of my host families where shocked as well, but I knew I had found something I was ready to die for.

So with the help of friends and family (Debbie Foley, Kwame Amoateng, Samuel Labi, Kristen Tetteh, Catherine Miller, Shelli Dean, and Sam and Kit Kollmeyer), One Kingdom Foundation was established through which the vision I saw in Florida is being fulfilled.

The vision behind One Kingdom Foundation is to create a platform through which we can speak to kids in middle school and high school through a different variety of programs that will inspire, equip, and empower them to live their dreams. Through soccer, clinics, inspirational speaking, mentorship programs, and sports-related programs, I knew I could make a difference in the lives of our youth, and I didn't waste any time. During my time in Seattle, I held soccer clinics at Microsoft, spoke at many middle schools, high schools, and colleges—and our programs were well received.

I eventually enrolled in the John C. Maxwell Team, a certification program that trains people how to speak, coach, and train others. I speak at many events and facilitate leadership seminars. Starting One Kingdom Foundation and enrolling in the John Maxwell Team really empowered me to do what I've always wanted to do: serve people, inspire people, equip people, and empower people to do more, believe more, and maximize their potential.

Making this dream of establishing my own nonprofit couldn't have been possible without the incredible dedication, commitment, and service mentality of many people who came alongside me and believed in my vision. We are partnering with other organizations and are doing a great work around the world to provide scholarship to students to help them realize their dreams.

The vision for One Kingdom Foundation is to build a residential leadership academy in Ghana. There are too many gifted young boys and girls who don't get the opportunity to realize their dreams. One of the great tragedies of poverty is that you are trapped in hopelessness. With no opportunity for vision, the pain and depression and suffering of poverty does not allow a person to see, because they are constricted by what is immediate and desperate. Even though the seed of greatness is in every human being, poverty and a lack of resources can trap their seed.

ONE KINGDOM FOUNDATION
KING'S LEADERSHIP ACADEMY

I was one of the lucky few who was given the opportunity to be in an environment where I could see a vision of a life better than the environment I was born in. And that's exactly the environment I want to provide for the youth in Ghana. Because I saw a vision of myself becoming a professional soccer player, it protected me from doing drugs, joining a gang, or going on a path that could lead me to a painful and unfulfilling future.

When fully completed, the leadership academy will be equipped with state-of-the-art facilities such as dormitories, classrooms, a library, a health center, a soccer field, an auditorium, and more. I want it to be an environment where young people can come and dream, a place where they can learn what true leadership is all about and how to maximize their full potential. After three years at our academy, we will help prepare them for college, either in Africa or the US.

As we work patiently in establishing the leadership academy in Ghana, my hope is to continue to share the vision with as many people as I can around the world.

ABOUT THE AUTHOR

Michael Tetteh was born in the Volta Region of Ghana. His soccer career began early in life playing for the Right to Dream Academy in Ghana before moving to Santa Barbara, California, on a full scholarship to attend Dunn High School in the Santa Ynez Valley, and then attending University of California Santa Barbara on a soccer scholarship. Michael's professional career began when he signed a generation Adidas contract with Major League Soccer and then was drafted by the Seattle Sounders.

Less than a year after being drafted, Michael took the field against European powerhouse Manchester United and competed against the world-class players he once idolized as a child back in Ghana. Despite achieving his dream of playing professional soccer, Michael stepped away from the game after two seasons to pursue his passion for educating and inspiring others.

Michael became a certified John C. Maxwell leadership coach and speaker and leads businesses to set smart goals and overcome tremendous odds. Michael's unique approach to leadership combines body, mind, and spirit to create harmony in the workplace. Audiences love Michael's energetic approach to teaching leadership techniques.

Michael founded One Kingdom Foundation, a nonprofit organization that seeks to be a catalyst for a new generation of African leaders with honorable character. The vision for the One Kingdom Foundation is building leadership education for low-income kids to discover their gifts and make a difference in their world.

To get involved, visit www.mtetteh.com

ACKNOWLEDGMENTS

Nothing worthwhile in life has ever been accomplished without the effort of many gifted individuals who are willing to contribute their experiences, gifts, and passions toward a common goal. This book is a product of many individuals whose ideas, support, and work have provided me with life-changing knowledge. I would like to acknowledge everyone who contributed and supported me. Without your help, this project would never have been finished.

I want to thank God for never giving up on me when I was told that I would never make it as a professional soccer player.

Thank you to my beautiful, gifted, intelligent, fantastic, and precious wife Kristen Tetteh. Your love, patience, wisdom, and belief in whom God created me to be is overwhelming. My accomplishments are yours as well, and I couldn't imagine doing this life with someone else. Love you forever.

Many thanks to my extended family in Santa Barbara, California; Ketchum, Idaho; and Seattle, Washington, who have supported me since moving to the US at the age of fifteen.

To my best friend, Waid Ibrahim, whose friendship, commitment, and accountability have guided me to finish this book. I'm truly grateful.

A massive thank you to all those who supported this self-publishing effort with your generous donations through my Kickstarter campaign. A special thanks to Larry Eddings, Kristi and Jesse Nelson, and Nelson Campbell for their generous show of support.

None of this, of course, would be smooth sailing without my writing support; Alice Sullivan and the Made For Success Publishing team. Thank you for your incredible gift and skill of bringing the best out of me. This work could not have been completed without you as you continually demonstrated the very principle of this book—using and sharing your gift. I'm forever grateful and will always remember your contribution though your gift.

SPECIAL
ACKNOWLEDGMENTS

Benjamin Franklin once said, "To the generous mind, the heaviest debt is that of gratitude, when it is not in our power to repay it."

When I was drafted by the Seattle Sounders, I met my friend and brother Steve Zakuani who took me under his wing, mentored me, and introduced me to the work of Dr. Myles Munroe. After reading the first book Steve gave me by Dr. Munroe, I went online and bought forty-nine more books by him and read every single one. I spent thousands of hours listening to his audios, YouTube messages, and streaming online videos of his teachings. Both Steve and Dr. Munroe taught me many things that helped me discover my true sense of significance and potential, and that increased my awareness and oneness with God.

As you read this book, you're going to find their insights and ideas reflected throughout, because their lives and work led me to a new awareness, which empowered me to transform and transcend the opinions and circumstances of my life. The difference that both Steve and Dr. Munroe made in my life is immeasurable, and I will always be grateful for that. A debt of gratitude is what I owe you. I will continue to pass on the legacy you have shown me.

ENDNOTES

1   "Bad Perm to Teenage CEO: Update with Jasmine Lawrence," Where Are They Now? Oprah Winfrey Network, https://www.youtube.com/watch?v=fv2w5NBTC8c.
2   Words from Solomon.
3   Genesis 1:26.
4   Paraphrased example from Myles Munroe, *Understanding Your Potential.*
5   *Strong's Concordance,* Hebrew 5730.
6   Delatorro McNeal II, *Caught Between a Dream and a Job* (Excel Books, 2008).
7   Myles Munroe, *Overcoming Crisis.*
8   Ecclesiastes 11:6 NIV.
9   Richard Dawkins, *The Selfish Gene* (Oxford University Press, 1979, pp. 2–3).
10 Genesis 1:26 NIV.
11 Proverbs 16:1.
12 Author has expanded upon four leadership ideas by John C. Maxwell, *The 21 Irrefutable Laws of Leadership Workbook* (Thomas Nelson Publishers, 2007).

CPSIA information can be obtained at www.ICGtesting.com
Printed in the USA
LVOW07s0428301215

468228LV00001B/1/P